Slayers

VOL. 3: THE GHOST OF SAIRAAG

WRITTEN BY
HAJIME KANZAKA

ILLUSTRATED BY
RUI ARAIZUMI

HAMBURG // LONDON // LOS ANGELES // TOKYO

Slayers Vol. 3: The Ghost of Sairaag
Written by Hajime Kanzaka
Illustrated by Rui Araizumi

Translation - Jeremiah Bourque
English Adaptation - Kelly Sue DeConnick
Copy Editor - Lonnee Hamilton
Associate Editor - Peter Ahlstrom
Design and Layout - James Lee
Cover Design - Kyle Plummer

Editor - Nicole Monastirsky
Digital Imaging Manager - Chris Buford
Pre-Press Manager - Antonio DePietro
Production Managers - Jennifer Miller and Mutsumi Miyazaki
Art Director - Matt Alford
Managing Editor - Jill Freshney
VP of Production - Ron Klamert
Editor-in-Chief - Mike Kiley
President and C.O.O. - John Parker
Publisher and C.E.O. - Stuart Levy

A  Novel

TOKYOPOP Inc.
5900 Wilshire Blvd. Suite 2000
Los Angeles, CA 90036

E-mail: info@TOKYOPOP.com
Come visit us online at www.TOKYOPOP.com

ISBN: 1-59532-579-4

First TOKYOPOP printing: March 2005
10 9 8 7 6 5 4 3 2 1
Printed in the USA

CONTENTS

1: YOU SCRATCH MY FACE, AND I'LL SLASH YOURS

There they were, standing right in front of us—lined up like an illustration out of a fairy tale: ten knights in shining armor. The sun gleamed luminously all around them, bouncing off the tips of their blades, so blindingly bright that the silver metal began to glow white. It was downright dazzling.

Gourry and I sighed, knowing that we both shared the same thought: *what a bunch of dorks.*

"At last we have found you, villains!" their leader announced, extending his index finger in our direction. *Doesn't he know it's rude to point?*

Here we go again. . . . We'd been running into groups of "heroes" just like these all too often lately.

"You—the Foul and Notorious Criminals Lina Inverse and Gourry Gabriev! Hark ye! I give thee notice that thy wickedness endeth here!"

Wow. Try saying that five times fast! He giveth uth notith that our wickedneth endeth here, huh?

The wind buffeted my mantle back as Sir Dork-a-lot prattled on. And on. And on. And on . . .

. . . And on some more! There was no point in interrupting. He wasn't going to listen to a "foul and notorious criminal" like me, anyway.

How did we get here, exactly? Well, it all started days before . . .

***

Clever girl that I am, I realized that I'd been captured the moment that I—uh—regained consciousness.

Yep, captured. Definitely captured. Definitely.

Oh, shush. *You* try thinking of something complex and clever the next time *your* limbs are bound up and aching and your head is throbbing like you've got an ogre dancing between your ears! And a gag! Did I mention I was *gagged*, too?!

At least the stone floor felt cool on my cheek. Not that clean-and-happy-other-side-of-the-pillow kind of cool, but considering that the room was muggy and damp and smelled like toxic mold, it wasn't an entirely unpleasant kind of cool, either. Near as I could tell we were in some sort of warehouse, someplace used for storing . . . mildew, maybe?

I looked around, hoping I'd spy something that would help me make more sense of the situation. I spotted two men—guards, presumably—staring at me from across the room. They were standing near what looked like it might have been a well, and each was armed with a crude club.

"Good morning, sunshine."

Who said that? I turned. *Gourry!*

Even bound hand and foot and stripped of his famous sword, he was still the same old Gourry: pretty as a painting and dumb as a zombie.

What? Okay, fine, I admit it! I exaggerate: the truth is that Gourry is very smart—*compared to a zombie*. Better? Look, Gourry is probably the best swordsman I've ever seen, but he isn't gonna win any prizes for his mental prowess. You know what I'm saying?

And—okay, I'll admit it—there was something kind of funny about seeing him all tied up. *Heh heh.*

I wonder why they didn't make him *wear a gag. I'd really have gotten a kick out of that. I mean, here we are, both tied up and I'm the one—Gahhhhh!*

What was I snickering about?! We were in trouble!

"Ntnnmh! Nmh!" Suddenly panicked, I struggled against my bonds. Alas, the more I squirmed, the worse things got.

"The girl's up," Guard A alerted Guard B.

"Ah . . . yep," confirmed Guard B, who didn't really know what he was supposed to do with that information. "You know . . . she really doesn't look the type," he mused.

Doesn't look WHAT *type?*

"And *that* is exactly why she's dangerous." Guard A smirked like he was some kind of Lina Inverse expert. "Don't ya go letting yer guard down on account of her looks."

Guard B nodded sagely.

Oh, please.

"Hey fellas," Gourry piped up. "You guys mind filling us in on why exactly you're holding us here?" He kept his tone light, like he was asking for the time of day.

And yet, A and B looked startled and pathetically . . . well, *pathetic.*

"Just who do ya think yer trying ta fool—" Guard A's eyes narrowed as he growled and clenched his club.

Reactionary nutjobs.

"Easy now," Guard B interceded.

"Yeah, okay," Guard A toned it down a notch, begrudgingly.

That would have been a good time for me to diplomatically diffuse the situation with my charm and wit—and I would have done so, too, if it hadn't been for that stupid gag in my mouth.

Guard A let his gaze creep in my direction. *Creep* being the operative word, as his look took a turn toward the lecherous.

Ew . . . what's with the stare, you perv?

"Kind of a waste, handing a girl like that over to the law, donchathink?"

Oh, ew ew ew! How did I know something like this was coming?

I mean, it's true: I am in possession of an intoxicating cocktail of physical attributes that together could be described as beautiful, or even irresistible, or—worst case— "kinda hot, for a flat girl." Still, a gentleman wouldn't *leer.*

Wait a minute! Hand me over to the law?!

I've been called some awful things in my time: Bandit Slayer, King of Hades—(I never really understood *that* one;

should I be offended?)—but those are the names that the bad guys call me because they're scared.

There is absolutely no reason whatsoever that I should be on the wrong side of the law!

Unless . . .

Gourry!

Oh, sure—he *seemed* like a nice guy, but how could I know for sure? We'd only been traveling together for a few months, and I really didn't know *that* much about him. Maybe there was some nefarious reason he never talked about himself. Maybe he was hiding something shady in his past? Ah, yes. That had to be it. It was all Gourry's fault. I became quite sure of it.

So then, why wasn't El Creepo staring at Gourry instead of me, huh?

"What did you do *this* time?" Gourry asked me, obviously at odds with my theory.

Me? Gourry, I'm crushed! How could you not trust me, after everything we've been through together?

It would have been fun to have faked a few tears and berated him for doubting me, but I couldn't sob properly with that gag in my mouth.

Bummer . . .

"What do you mean, a waste?" B asked, his tone suggesting he already knew the answer.

"After we hand her over, it's only a matter of time 'til her neck comes off her shoulders, right? So if'n we were to, uh, *mess around with her* a little bit, who would mind?"

Me! Yoo hoo! Over here! I would mind! I would mind quite a bit—thankyouverymuch!

If it wasn't me and it wasn't Gourry, then it had to be a case of mistaken identity, right? Nothing else made any sense! But since, "Oh gee, fellas, you've got the wrong gal," probably wasn't going to throw cold water on A's plans, I still had a pressing problem on my hands.

"I'm not so sure that's a good idea."

So B was on my side! *Yay, B!* Okay, sure, it sounded more like fear than any moral compunction, but considering the circumstances, I didn't want to pick nits. I had my champion.

You tell him, B! Show A who's boss! You go, B!

"Fine," said A. "You stand guard, then. If she tries anything funny, beat her to death."

"Yeah . . . yeah, okay. I s'pose."

No! No, not "I s'pose"!! C'mon B! Don't give in!

"Relax, would ya? I'm not gonna *untie* her or anything. It's better this way."

11

"Heh, I hadn't thought of that. Um, in that case maybe I'll, uh—"

Oh, nuh-UH! Don't change teams on me! I'm depending on you!

B smiled. It was not the kind of smile I was hoping for.

What are you doing smiling with the perv?! Hey, now! Stay away from me!

They both came at me. I squirmed and kicked, but tied up the way I was, I couldn't put up much of a fight. Let's be honest: even if I *hadn't* been tied up, I don't exactly excel in the arena of brute force. Of course, being both a swordfighter and a sorceress, I could more than even the odds with my spells, but with a gag in my mouth, I couldn't defend myself at all.

Guard A grabbed my chin with his very large hand. I wished I could spit.

"Don't like it, huh? Thought ya were gonna get away with all yer evildoin' scot-free, did ya?"

What evildoin'?!

"C'mon then." A pulled me closer to his face . . .

"That's enough!" Gourry warned. He was still tied up, but he spoke with such authority that both guards automatically took a half step back. "If you so much as lay a hand on her . . ."

For one glorious moment, the two guards froze.

Gotta hand it to you, Gourry. That's some powerful will you've got there.

The room was tense—each of us still and silent, waiting to see who'd make the next move. Then . . .

"Heh," Guard A smiled, shattering my hopes.

Damn! The great Lina Inverse at the mercy of villains such as these! This sucks.

The worst part was that I didn't even know why we were being held—or by whom!

"W-we're not afraid of you!" B said, making an effort to sound like he had a spine.

Your voice is quivering. Nobody's buying the tough-guy act, jerkface.

"If we so much as lay a hand on her, what?" A asked. "What d'ya think yer gonna do about it? Yer all tied up!"

"If you so much as a lay a hand on that girl," Gourry repeated calmly.

"You'll what?" A was laughing now.

". . . You'll catch what she *has*."

A stopped laughing. Gourry smiled.

I wished I could kill them all with my mind.

Slowly at first, the two men backed away. Their bodies displayed the physical tension born of Trying Very Hard Not to Panic. They looked like they very much wanted to wash their hands. With scrub brushes. And bleach.

My eyes narrowed to small points.

"I, um . . ." A was trying to conceal the depth of his horror and he wasn't doing a very good job. "I think we might just play 'er safe. Stick to what we know, y'know?"

"Y-yeah, safe is good. I like safe." There was a pregnant pause, and then they both laughed like it had all been some silly joke. Their laughter resolved in a pair of long, deep sighs.

"What say we step outside?" A asked B.

"Good call, good call. It's a little moist in here. Wouldn't want to catch anything, you know what I'm saying?"

Oh, please . . .

They each shot me a glance as they made their way outside.

"Whew. I thought they'd never leave," Gourry chuckled.

Grrr!

I glared as I silently crawled over to him, on my belly, like a worm.

"Oh, come on, Lina! You're not mad, are you? It was the best thing I could think of under the circumstances."

I ooched closer.

"The important thing is that you're safe, right? I mean, come on! I saved you! Lina—wait, don't!"

As hard as I could, I smashed both feet into his face.

I feel much better now, thanks.

"You didn't have to kick me," Gourry whined just before pulling my gag out with his teeth.

"No, I didn't *have to*, but it was my pleasure! You couldn't come up with anything better than suggesting I was *infectious?!*"

"It was the first thing I thought of!"

I glared.

"What was I supposed to do? Let those guys work you over while I thought up something more flattering?"

"No! I mean . . ." I had to admit he had a point.

"See . . . ?"

"All right. Okay . . . well . . . fine! You might be right—*this* time!"

That was my version of an apology.

"Is that what you call an apology?" Gourry roared.

Duh. Hold it down; the nutjobs are gonna hear you.

"Seriously Lina, you can tell me the truth: were you raised by wolves?"

"Oh, shut up! Never mind! Let's just focus on getting out of here, okay? This ought to do it . . . Bram Fang!"

Bram Fang—in case you're not familiar with it—is a spell that shoots wind arrows at a target, shredding it, in effect, with air. Well, actually, that might be overstating the case a little. A target would have to be pretty flimsy for Bram Fang to shred it. It *would* scratch up a human opponent's skin, but wouldn't do any damage at all to a person wearing, say, leather armor. The sorceresses who taught me Bram Fang suggested it be used as a molester repellant—and it does come in handy in that regard—but I figured out that if you cast it several times on a single point, it's strong enough to cut though something like, oh, rough-hewn rope, for instance.

Once I'd freed Gourry, he returned the favor—the old-fashioned way, of course.

"We need to find our swords," he said as he helped me to my feet.

"Yep. And then we need to find out what's going on."

"Agreed."

We'd arrived in the village—which was situated right on the edge of a mountain range—just the night before. Though the villagers had greeted us with a certain amount of hostility, we honestly hadn't paid much attention to it.

See, the two of us had been traveling more or less along the Hawk's Highway, a thoroughfare that had been open roughly five years. We'd kept fairly close to the beaten path, but even so, each time we passed through a village, we got that prickly feeling that meant we were being watched.

It had been the same story in this village, but we'd arrived late and tired, and we weren't easily spooked, so we rented a room in the first inn we saw.

We ate supper and soon after the Sandman came for us with a vengeance. Next thing we knew, we'd been captured.

"This is the part where you're going to explain—slowly and clearly—why you were holding us," Gourry whispered into Guard A's ear from behind. He was twisting the guy's arms behind his back as I glared into his eyes.

"Do not raise your voice," I warned. "If you do—"

"Have merrrrrrccccccy!" Guard A sobbed and shrieked, writhing in pain.

Wow. That was easy.

Guard B, who was on the ground right next to the well, was silent.

Gourry rested a fingertip on the nape of A's neck, poking him a little bit. "Don't be such a crybaby," he said. I think he was embarrassed for the guy. "Hey, now. Your buddy's not dead or anything. He just fainted, that's all," he explained in a tone usually reserved for children.

They were pathetic—make no mistake—but we went ahead and tied them up just to be on the safe side. And also because turnabout is fair play.

***

It was dark. The stars in the sky and a sliver of moon as thin as a wire provided the only light. The silhouettes of the townspeople's homes were outlined against the dim horizon. Not a single light burned in a single window. That meant the villagers were long asleep.

"So, what's the story? What did you want with us, huh?" I asked.

"Wh-what did we want? The bounty, of course! Ya have a huge bounty on yer heads, ya know!"

Gourry and I both checked to see if the other had any idea where that may have come from. We didn't.

"Mistaken identity," I surmised. "Well, probably. I'm Lina Inverse, and this is—"

"G-Gourry Gabriev . . . or something like that," A mumbled.

Huh?

I looked to Gourry once more. It didn't make any more sense to him than it did to me. Well, okay . . . someone must have committed some evil deed in our names, leading to a bounty to be placed on our heads due to our notoriety. It was only a guess, but it wasn't something we could ignore either way.

"So who put up the bounty, anyway?" Gourry asked

"I-I have no idea . . . b-but the warrant said the reward was only good if'n you was captured alive," A offered.

Only if captured alive?

That was more bizarre. Who would want Gourry and me so much they'd specify that we had to be captured alive? At any rate, it seemed futile to question those clowns any further.

So I changed the subject. "You took our swords. So where are they?"

"The—um—the village chieftain's house . . . th-that's where we left 'em, anyway. I think they're still there."

Fear had loosened him up, and our man was proving to be quite the talker.

"Great. Where's the village chieftain's house, then?"

He didn't hesitate to answer. Now, if we'd been *real* villains, he'd have just placed his chieftain's life in danger. At least we knew what kind of man we were dealing with at that point. He was weak to the strong, strong to the weak, and concerned for his own skin above all else.

Charming . . .

"All right, thanks then. You've been a great help, you toad. Gourry, let's go."

"Right." As Gourry released our former guard, he gave the nape of his neck a short sharp thrust with his fingertip. It was a specialty move and enough to knock him out cold.

Sweet dreams, jerkface.

Leaving the two would-be molesters behind, we followed their directions to the chieftain's house.

"Be quiet," I told Gourry, as we approached the home.

"I couldn't raise my voice if I tried," Gourry whispered, shaking a little. Breaking and entering always did make him uneasy.

For his part, the old man didn't seem surprised he had guests. He sat up easily in bed, his lamplight brushing aside the darkness.

"Ah, yes. There you are," he said, sounding like he'd been expecting us.

We were fairly taken aback by that, to tell you the truth.

"We . . . we've come for our swords."

The old man gave a slow nod and graciously ignored my stuttering. "They are inside that closet on the topmost shelf," he said. "Take them and go."

Gourry searched the closet (of course, I couldn't have reached if I'd tried) and found our swords right where they were supposed to be.

"But . . . why?" was all I could think to ask.

"After hearing of your arrival, I ordered that your meal be drugged and you be disarmed and taken into custody. However, as I watched you sleep, I could not help but wonder if there had been some mistake."

Great minds think alike, old man.

"You do not have the aura of evildoers. While it is true, of course, that there are those in this world who can perform great misdeeds and appear the picture of innocence, they generally have something in their aura to indicate that they should not be trusted." The old man shook his head mournfully, "You do not."

"Pull open the drawer below the shelf where the swords were, please?" he instructed Gourry. "Yes, that one. As far as you can, please? Now, take out the paper you find there."

Gourry did as he was told and then tilted the lamp so that he and I could get a better look at the flyer.

"It's . . . it's . . ." Gourry and I were incredulous. The document we held was a wanted poster—for us! Worse yet, the reward being offered for three people was more than ten times what you might expect for five.

If we'd killed a king, we wouldn't have this much on our heads!

And lest there be any doubts as to our identities, they'd included our portraits—of course drawn to make us look like we'd just killed puppies in cold blood and had thoroughly enjoyed the deed. But despite the foul expressions, those were definitely our faces. And below them, our names: Lina Inverse and Gourry Gabriev.

Huh . . .

What *really* surprised me, though, was the *third* wanted person. The three of us had only been involved in one incident together . . .

Wait, that couldn't mean . . . could it?

"Hey, Lina, this guy . . ." Gourry pointed to the third face on the poster. "I could swear I've seen him somewhere before."

Smart for a zombie, huh?

"Gourry, how the *hell* do you manage to forget someone with a face like *that?*" I was genuinely skeptical.

"The bounty was the problem," the chieftain interrupted. "For that sum, the entire village could live in luxury for the remainder of the year. How could I say to my tired people, 'I suspect these *villains* are innocents?' "

That wouldn't have gone over well. I could see his point.

"There is something else you should know: the bounty is being offered by a man of . . . well, though I do not know him personally, he is a man of noblest reputation."

"You know who put out the bounty, then?!" I couldn't wait to hear this one.

"He is one of the great sages of this age," the chieftain nodded. "The Wandering Sage, Rezo the Red Priest. Surely you have heard of him, have you not?"

Oh. No. Way.

My jaw was hanging open, and there was no way I could explain it to him.

Even if I'd been willing to go through it again—and I wasn't—telling the whole story would have taken too long. Besides, if I'd heard it from someone else, *I* wouldn't have believed it.

Here's the short version:

Two months ago—right around the time Gourry and I first met—a certain item came into my hands that a certain group of unsavory fellows had their sights on.

This aforementioned group of unsavories was led by a man bearing the name of the great sage Rezo the Red Priest, and his then-loyal righthand man, the magic-weilding swordsman Zelgadiss.

(There was no doubt in my mind whatsoever that the third portrait on the wanted poster was that of Zelgadiss, by the way.)

After several battles, Zelgadiss betrayed Rezo, but the item fell into Rezo's hands.

The Red Priest responded by transforming himself into an apocalyptic Mazoku. Sure, you know—what else would he do?

But, in a fearsome battle that nearly destroyed us all—and the rest of the world for that matter—Gourry, Zelgadiss, and I were finally able to defeat the Mazoku. So, long story short-ish: Rezo *couldn't* be alive. And since dead people can't pay bounties, that warrant *had* to be a fake.

"Well, this warrant's no longer valid," I said. "The Red Priest was reported dead two months ago." Of course, I didn't add that *we* defeated him. *That* would have caused more trouble since Rezo's true nature was still unknown to the general populace. Most believed him to be a righteous (if not downright holy) man.

"Two months ago?" the old man eyed me doubtfully. "This warrant was delivered only about a week ago. The bounty itself seems to have been declared only one week prior to that. Perhaps there is some mistake."

Two weeks? Gourry and I looked at each other. *Couldn't be . . . could it?*

"Well, do you know where *this* Red Priest is at the moment, then?" I asked, wondering if we might be dealing with an impostor.

"I do not." The old man shook his head. "However, if you truly are innocent, go west to Crimson City. You can ask for more details there, as that is where the bounty is to be paid. It is in Crimson City that you may find the Red Priest and resolve this . . . *misunderstanding.*"

I was beginning to doubt that it really was a misunderstanding, but I nodded anyway.

"Misunderstandings give rise to such sadness . . ." the old man mumbled, sighing heavily as he looked into the distance.

Poor old guy. I wonder what he's remembering. But we didn't have time to ponder the chieftain's broken heart.

"Thank you, sir," Gourry said quietly. Obviously, the old man had made an impression on him as well.

"We don't wish to be a bother to you any longer," I said, offering a little bow. "So if you'll please excuse us."

"Of course." The old man nodded.

And with that, Gourry and I headed for Crimson City.

***

By the time we broke camp the next morning, we were famished. We'd been up most of the night, putting as much distance between ourselves and our former captors as possible before closing our eyes again. We kept moving while we ate a late breakfast.

"So what do you think this is all about?" I asked. "I mean, I'm not holding you to anything concrete. But if you had to guess . . ."

"You mean about Rezo the Red Priest being alive?"

I nodded.

"Well, there's a few things it could be," Gourry said, his arms folded.

I followed a bit behind him and allowed him to compose his thoughts. The stone-paved highway stretched out before us as far as the eye could see. Green-covered mountain peaks rose up from the horizon. A gentle breeze blew across the grassy fields. I could hear birds singing somewhere nearby.

Um . . . hello?

"Gourry . . . you haven't thought about this at all yet, have you?"

"Nope." He smiled brightly as he scratched his face.

Nope?!

"If you never think about anything at all, your brain's gonna turn into tartar sauce!" I shouted, for reasons that make no more sense to me than they do to you.

"Huh? What's tartar sauce?" Gourry asked, missing the point entirely.

The zombies are gaining on you, Gourry. Grrr.

"It's true that there are several obvious possibilities," I went on, ignoring the question. "The one that makes the most sense is that the Rezo offering the bounty is an impostor. Some of Rezo's underlings might be using his name to try to take revenge on us for killing his master. That's on the top of my list of possibilities, anyway.

"Of course, if that were the case, just sullying our names wasn't going to be good enough; a revenge-seeker would want to destroy us with his own hands—and that would explain why the poster specified that we were to be delivered alive.

"Another possibility is simple incompetence. There was a gap of several days between the time Zelgadiss and I ran away and when we met you again, so Rezo could have told a minion to put out a warrant on us during that time. And then for some reason—maybe government bureaucracy—it wasn't issued until it was almost two months later—

"No, that's no good. There'd be no point in capturing us alive . . ." I was thinking out loud.

"There's one other possibility," Gourry said, sounding alarmingly serious.

I looked in his eyes and I knew what he meant. There *was* one other possibility, my least favorite of all possible explanations . . .

"*Rezo the Red Priest* is alive," I muttered quietly toward the cloudless blue sky. "If that is the case . . . we're not gonna win this time."

***

Despite my overwhelming desire to slaughter Sir Dork-a-lot in vengeance for his subjecting us to a boring lecture fulleth of "thees" and "thous" and "thines," we were not murderers, after all, so he and his corny crew would be allowed to live.

That didn't mean I wasn't going to blacken their bodies entirely with ash, however. A girl's gotta have some fun.

Ever since we left that village, we've had more groups of "heroes" trying to delivereth "judgment" every day. And it was still six days 'til Crimson City! According to my rough calculations, if the number of heroes continued to rise at the current rate, we'd be facing three-hundred-man teams by the day of our arrival.

That would suck.

I tried my best not to think about it. I was feeling as gloomy as a demon as it was.

"Is this our destiny; we, the Eight Silver Knights of the Duchy of Lenos?"

This knight does not know when to shut up.

They still thought we were bad guys—after we'd gone easy on them! If we'd been *real* bad guys, they would've had some serious attack spells coming their way, and they'd be much worse off, but they didn't look like they could even tell the difference.

I tried to focus on keeping my spirits up by patting myself on the back.

Congratulations, Lina! Once again, you've shown the necessary level of mercy so as not to kill any of them. That includes accidental deaths and untreatable wounds. Yay, you! Lina the Merciful!

Don't laugh. We have a saying back home: Sometimes a show of mercy is required to smash a boulder. And it's true! You know, there are a lot of powerful and reckless people running around in this world who don't understand that. I—uh—might have taken a while to really understand it myself.

(Maybe this would be a good time to mention that my older sister back home is a bit calmer than I am, and . . . no, maybe I shouldn't mention it. I'm not sure how she'd feel about seeing it in print. Never mind. Move along. Nothing to see here.)

"Lo and alas! If only t'were ten years ago, villains . . ."

I glared at the yappy guy as I chanted a little spell, Bomb Sprid!

KA-BOOM!

"Dyaaaa!" The seven knights screamed as they were battered by my merciful attack.

Huh? Weren't there eight? Well, either way was fine, really.

"Lina, I've been thinking . . . do you know what the word *mercy* means?" Gourry was looking at me like I'd just slapped his mommy.

"Of course I do! If I hadn't shown mercy just now, the only thing left of those seven—er, eight?—would be pieces of flaming armor!"

"Well, sure, they're still *alive*, but . . ." Gourry's voice trailed off as he watched, with sympathetic eyes, the knights rain back down to the ground.

They were screaming and shouting half-incomprehensible things like, "We're not ready!" and "Not yet! Not here!" and "Hangeth on, fellows! Do not die!" before crashing unceremoniously back to earth. Some of them even bounced.

Yeah, okay, maybe I overdid it just a little.

"You know, they're not bad guys," Gourry reminded me. He sounded tired. "Couldn't you just . . ."

I tut-tutted and waved my finger at him. "Hey, I'm using mild attack spells, okay?"

Gourry let out a long sigh.

We didn't talk much the rest of the night.

***

I didn't *toss* so much as I *twisted* and turned, unable to sleep even a wink.

Luckily, even while on the run from the law, we could slip into a large city, get what we needed and lodge in one of the various inns.

But still, for some reason, I had a dull pain in my chest. The feeling had grown stronger over the past several days, most noticeably whenever we were at an inn. I could barely sleep at all, night or day.

In my heart of hearts, I understood the cause.

I thought about Gourry, who was probably still asleep in the next room. It was the first time I'd had this feeling since we'd met.

Maybe he's still awake?

The pain in my chest grew stronger as I pondered him.

Sigh . . .

I gave up on sleep and got out of bed. Gently, I stroked the cold thin wall that separated our rooms. He had to be asleep. I pressed my ear to the surface, but couldn't hear him breathe.

He's probably sleeping soundly, so . . .

"Sleeping!" I got so excited I said it aloud. Why didn't I think of this before?

With that, I fired my spell through the wall. Not even the cry of a banshee or the roar of a dragon would wake him before morning.

All right!!

Satisfied at last, I smiled and began to dress: white robe, black trousers—check! Bandanna on the forehead, boots, long gloves—check! Dragon scale shoulder guards and my dead-of-night black mantle, plus my short sword on my hip—check, check and check!

Armoring complete!

Hee hee . . . hee hee hee . . .

A grin spread across my face. This would cure me of the ache in my chest!

Yes! This is it!

Ever since I'd met Gourry, I hadn't made time for bandit-hunting. I'd been denying my true self! And simply put, I just couldn't take it anymore. As one of those knights might say, it was a very foul morning to be-eth a bandit.

I finished dressing and headed to the dining hall where some of the other lodgers were trading gossip about bandit groups operating nearby. It seemed I wasn't the only one who was getting impatient.

I was able to get a rough idea of where the bandit hideout was, based on what I heard at the inn.

Only a fool runs off to get lost along the way.

I snuck out into the forest under the cover of night and ran along what seemed more like a game trail than a road. There was no mistake, though; I was on the right path.

Before long, I spied red and orange flames coming from the direction of some ruins.

A bandit campfire!

There were a number of them gathered around the flames. They bore scimitars and wore black tunics. They'd been drinking, and every once in a while one of them would whoop it up.

Drunken bandits cavorting around a campfire . . . nice and *original, guys.*

No doubt they'd have guards posted not far from the open fire. The ruins behind them looked to be their stronghold.

It would've been fun just to charge forward and blow them all away, but using the more powerful attack spells would destroy the ruins and—here's the important part— bury any treasure inside, out of reach. So the challenge was to lure them out.

I removed my shoulder guards and short sword, wrapping them thoroughly in my mantle. Holding them in both hands with a devotion that might be called religious,

I began to backtrack along the path. Then, taking a deep breath . . .

"Help meee!" I screamed at the top of my lungs, and I ran as fast as I could.

When all eyes were on me, I performed a spectacular pratfall, landing right between their guards. I never let go of my bundled mantle—of course.

"Help . . . please . . . help me!" I whelped, clinging to the closest bandit and breathing heavily.

It seemed the thing to do.

"H-hey now! What happened?" asked the bandit I was draped across. They were all perplexed.

Good.

"He's coming! He's—please! I have to get away! He'll kill me! He'll kill me for sure, I know he will!" I spat out fragmented, nonsensical lines as fast as I could come up with them.

The guards looked at each other, trying to decide what to do. They weren't a decisive bunch. Finally, one blurted out, "I'm gonna take a little look around!" and ran off into the woods.

I was wrapped in the closest man's arms, shivering weakly and muttering words that were utterly incomprehensible to normal people.

That is to say, I was muttering a quick attack spell, Mega Brand.

BOOM! A nearby explosion sent a spectacular roar into the air.

"What the—?!" The group fell into a panic.

"It's him! He's here!" I called out, pointing toward the trees.

"Where?!" someone shouted.

"Who's here?!" another joined the chorus.

Quietly, I began my next spell.

"What's going on here?!" the fellow who appeared to be the bandit leader demanded. A moment later, the rest of the crew from inside the ruins came out to investigate the commotion. I counted ten men.

I continued my havoc-wreaking with the Vice Flare spell.

GA-GA-GAB-SHOOOOON! Fire broke out everywhere, spreading to bottles of booze and causing more explosions.

Nice.

"What the—?!"

"The hell you say . . . !"

It was beautiful chaos. Having no idea what was going on, the bandits bolted for the woods. Some meant to flee, some meant to fight, but none remembered to stick around and guard their booty.

So . . . everything they had was mine. Fair and square. You snooze, you lose, losers.

Inside the ruins was indeed a proper treasure chest. It was pretty full, almost the sort you'd expect from a merchant guild.

Hee hee, there's even more here than I thought!

More than half the bandits had been slain in the process of creating the huge uproar that made the others flee. So I felt pretty secure poking around. I spread out my mantle and began pulling a hemp rope lined with linen out of a hidden pocket. By running the rope along the edge and tying the ends together just so . . .

Voila! A simple knapsack!

Then it was just a matter of deciding which and how much to take. Cramming everything of value into the sack would make it so heavy that the cord would break. If I got greedy, then I'd lose everything! So, I was looking for the items with the most value per ounce—things like precious jewels, anything with artistic value, magic items . . .

I was poking through the rubble when an angry voice called out from behind me, "Hey! What are you doing in there?!"

Yikes!

I almost jumped out of my skin.

If the opponent had been a simple bandit, then one attack spell would've spelled t-h-e e-n-d. However, I turned around very, very slowly and the face I saw was, sadly, just the one I'd feared.

"Oh, hey! Er, hi there! What a pleasant surprise it is to see you, Gourry! What brings you out this way?" I put my hands to my mouth, making a big show of my surprise. I also blinked a lot. That always helps.

"What am *I* doing here?" he said, not buying my act for a minute. "I'm trying to find out what you're up to."

"Little ole me? Tee hee. Why, it's a s-e-c-r-e-t."

"Knock it off, Lina."

Ulp . . . Well, if that's not gonna work . . .

I stuck out my chest and declared proudly, "I'm bandit hunting."

"I'm serious! Cut the act, Lina."

I'm serious, too! What am I supposed to say?

"Forget it!" I sighed. "Let's get out of here."

With a mutter under his breath, Gourry grabbed my hand and started yanking me along after him as he walked.

"H-hey, now! Wait! My treasure!" I protested. He wasn't stopping. "Come on! This is going just a little too far, don't you think?!"

Gourry continued dragging me behind him along the path back into the forest.

"What's too far about it?" he snapped, looking at me but not stopping.

Uh-oh. He's seriously pissed off.

"Running off into the woods—alone—in the middle of the night! Jeez, Lina! What were you thinking! *Were* you thinking at all?!"

"I was planning for a brighter future," I deadpanned. "Anyway, what's wrong with hunting bandits? They're lowlifes who make their living stealing from other people! If I let them do as they please, who knows who they'll rob next, what havoc they will surely wreak! Hey—I'm doing a public service, dammit!"

"Oh, right, okay—so this has nothing to do with taking their treasure?" He let out a heavy sigh.

"What am I supposed to do, just leave it there to rot? We don't know who the proper owners are, so it's not like we can just return it. If I leave it there, eventually some government is going to get their hands on it, and that's only going to cause more harm than good. At least if I take it and spend it, I'll be promoting the local economy," I pleaded.

"Do you even hear yourself?"

"Shouldn't you be asleep?!" I shrieked, exasperated. I didn't ask how he'd shirked off my sleeping spell. Oh, hell no. What was I, suicidal?

"Well, I was sleeping, but then I had to get up and go to the washroom. I heard sounds coming from your room, and by the time I got back to *my* room, I saw you out the window. You looked like you were using some kind of floating spell to get to the ground. Then you ran off!"

Ah. So that was it. That explained why I hadn't so much as heard him breathing.

Hmph. Dumb luck.

"In any event . . ." A voice from the darkness stopped us both cold.

Who said that?

I looked and listened hard. Insects buzzed faintly in the distance. Starlight seeped in softly through gaps in foliage. I couldn't see or hear anything unusual.

"How have you been?" the voice continued casually. It was coming from deep within a thicket.

Gourry's hand went to the hilt of his sword.

"I see some things haven't changed. You lack a certain subtly, you know." That time it sounded like it was coming from right behind us.

Impossible.

We still weren't detecting any presence. The two of us turned around, flustered. We were at a loss.

A red silhouette emerged from the darkness . . . a solitary priest wearing a robe as red as blood. His mantle fluttered softly in the wind. He was hooded, but I could see that both eyes were firmly shut. Even with his face mostly concealed, he was clearly . . .

"Rezo the Red Priest," I muttered as I stared, dumbfounded.

"It has been awhile, hasn't it? You two look rather well, considering," he said. There was no expression on his face. "Considering how tired you must be. Attacked by assassins day and night. It must be difficult."

"Yeah. *Someone* put a price on our heads." As I spoke, I realized something: even though the *form* of Rezo was right before us, I still couldn't sense his presence.

Under these circumstances, even he shouldn't be able to completely conceal his aura.

"A price? Ah yes, I prefer to think of those warrants as my *written invitation.* Currently, I am residing in the home of the High Priest of Sairaag."

Sairaag . . .

Sairaag was a city about five days' journey to the north. Though it was now known primarily as a city of magic, it was known as the City of Ghosts for a period after the destruction of the Demon Beast Zanaffar some one hundred years before. The tree, planted by the hero who had destroyed Zanaffar, had grown enormous and was the city's symbol. The city itself had blossomed as well. But, that was beside the point. How could Rezo be in Sairaag if he was also standing right before us?

"Vision," I whispered the name of the spell that was used to project an image of oneself over a very long distance, making it possible to communicate over miles; it was a rather convenient spell.

The thing was, Vision required a terminal—which could be another sorcerer—on the broadcast end. In other words, there had to be a sorcerer under Rezo's command close by.

"So you're trying to get us to go to Sairaag, huh?" Gourry spoke up.

"Come, or do not come," the Red Priest replied. "It is your choice. However, if you do not come, you will simply live the rest of your lives as fugitives."

"*Simply*, he says!" I couldn't help but laugh, bitterly. "I don't know about Gourry, but that wouldn't be simple for me."

"Me either," Gourry grumbled.

"I will await your company, then. And I look forward to that day when we may consider this matter *resolved*." And with that, his form vanished.

Gourry looked to me for an explanation.

"A transmission," I explained. My voice sounded grave, I'm sure.

"Indeed, it was transmitted!" Another voice called out from behind.

Once again we turned around, flustered, though this time the presence was not elusive or even difficult to perceive.

We faced a single figure, a man of medium build wearing a black mantle and hood, typical sorcerer's clothes. He also seemed to have large rubies embedded in the tips of his thumbs, which was in no way typical.

That sorcerer must've been the terminal—hiding here from the start, relaying the discussion with Rezo, just as I'd suspected.

I glared at the man. I could tell by his eyes he was third-rate.

"What's someone like *you* doing as Rezo's lackey?" I challenged.

"Cease your prattle, brat," he barked, then laughed. "The great Rezo need not concern himself with the likes of you. My name is Vrumugun—and as a service to my liege, I shall dispense with you here and now!"

Now, wait just a minute.

After Rezo went to all the trouble inviting us to Sairaag, this guy was going to completely ignore his master's wishes? It wasn't that it was sudden; it was that it was sudden and *stupid*.

This guy's stupid. Stupid guys are trouble.

"Buzz off, Sparky," I said, waving my hand at him dismissively. "It's great that you found us and everything— congratulations—but 'dispensing with us' is more than a little beyond your capabilities."

"I thank you for your kind congratulations, but you were not difficult to find, you know. Like a child, you seem unable to go more than a day or two without causing a ruckus. Your antics out here acted as something of a *beacon*."

Oh, excuse me? Did he just call me a child?

"You say my abilities are insufficient," he bellowed. "Let us test that theory!" As he finished, his right hand went behind his back. The next moment . . .

"Gah!" I swooped forward, ducking under the black object hurling toward my head.

With a dull sound, the trunk of the tree right behind me—which was about twice the thickness of one of Gourry's arms—snapped in two.

"A chain whip?!" Gourry identified the weapon immediately.

As the name suggests, a chain whip is an inelegant doohickey comprised of a chain and a small weight attached to its tip. As was just demonstrated, it is powerful, but in the hands of an amateur, far more dangerous to the user than a blade.

Vrumugun began casting a spell as he made a series of attacks with the chain whip.

That spell's rhythm . . . I recognize that. Fireball?!

Fireball is an attack spell that releases a ball of light, which explodes on impact, spreading flames throughout the area indiscriminately.

What the hell was that guy thinking, using fireball in the middle of a *forest?!* If the flames got out of control, he'd be on the menu at his own barbecue.

Grrr! Idiot! Incompetent! Reckless!

I began casting my counterattack.

"Fireball!" he shouted, and a crimson ball of light sprang forth from Vrumugun's left hand.

"Freeze Bullet!" I countered.

We both released our spheres and the two impacted squarely between us.

Shhhhrr-reeeep! There was a loud sound like something being ripped apart, then . . . nothing.

"What?! What did you do?" Vrumugun pouted like a baby.

Who's a child now, huh?

The spells' effects had been mutually negated, a little trick I'd discovered by accident while working on a job with another sorceress.

Let me take a moment here just to make sure you understand that casting a spell of the opposite element is *not* guaranteed to produce this effect. Depending on how you mix them together, the first spell's power can instead be greatly amplified. That is to say, just mixing a fireball and Freeze Bullet any old way could end up producing one hell of a fireball. Although researching the effects of combining various spells is an interesting field, it's far too large a job for any one person, even a super-genius sorceress like me. The sorceress with whom I'd worked on the matter had wandered off on her own a little while before I met Gourry. In any case, it's an area of specialized research, and average sorcerers don't know much about it. Vrumugun, for instance, was clueless.

He was so taken aback, in fact, that he was just standing there, not moving.

Gourry took advantage of this slip and knocked the chain whip out of Vrumugun's hand and high into the air.

"Curse you!" Vrumugun cried and he ran off in a panic. Gourry gave chase.

I began chanting my next spell.

The sorcerer reached behind his back like he might pull something else out, but Gourry beat him to it with a kick to the solar plexus.

"Guh!" The sorcerer's body folded as he cried out. Then I ended it.

"Elmekia Lance!" I shouted, and Vrumugun collapsed completely.

Elmekia Lance damages an opponent's mind. When used at its maximum power on a human being, the spell greatly debilitates the victim's intellect, often causing a shutdown similar to a coma or a very deep sleep.

But I cast the spell at less than maximum power by design. There were things I wanted to ask Vrumugun, and a comatose man wasn't likely to volunteer answers.

Just as I'd planned, he was flat on his back, effectively paralyzed. He wouldn't be able to make a physical attack or control a spell in his condition. But he was still conscious.

"If I wasn't so tired and grumpy, we would try this a hundred times and it would always end with you at my mercy," I said, gazing down into the sorcerer's face. "That's what happens when you overestimate your own strength."

Gourry stood beside me, on guard and paying close attention. He was ready to pound the Vrumbumpkin into the dirt if he tried anything funny. Because of his support, I was able to concentrate on direct interrogation.

"Who was that guy?" I demanded, with no pussyfooting around.

Vrumugun's creepy-thin eyebrows rose up in surprise. "What do you mean, who was that? Surely you know Lord Rezo?"

"We . . . *destroyed* . . . Rezo," I said, speaking slowly, pronouncing each word carefully so as to be understood, "a little over two months ago."

"That's just foolishness! If you did so, then who was that before you?"

"*I don't know*—that's why I'm asking you, you moron!" I replied.

At least we knew—for what it was worth—that this idiot believed he was working for the real Rezo.

"You speak nonsense! How could novices like you defeat *him?!*" He looked almost insulted.

Considering how easily we'd whupped his ass, he had no right to scoff. Novices, indeed!

"Oh *really?* In exactly what area do you find us lacking?"

Vrumugun looked me directly in the eyes and said, "Breasts."

I'm not sure precisely how far I sent him flying. Far, I promise you that. Very, very far.

***

Gourry and I returned to the inn just as night was changing to dawn. Then we passed yet another morning walking side by side along the highway. We draped a shroud over ourselves as our lazy man's form of disguise. We were short on sleep, but with our enemy knowing exactly where we were and exactly where we were going, it was best to keep on the move.

Vrumugun, by the way, had finally stopped flying when he collided with a tree. Sure, we could've cut him down at the time, but finishing off a completely incapacitated opponent just wasn't my style.

"So . . . what do you think, Gourry? About last night's 'Rezo,' I mean." My question seemed to send him deep into thought.

Don't hurt yourself there, buddy.

"To be honest, that face . . . well, it didn't feel like we were talking with a total stranger, you know?"

I knew. He certainly had a point. However . . .

"If it's not him, and it's not a total stranger, that only leaves one option, right?"

"You mean . . . a relative of some sort?"

"Okay, well, two options, then. I was thinking that it might be a copy of Rezo."

"A *copy?*" Gourry looked at me like I was drunk.

"Yeah, like a clone. You remember all the homunculi from Atlas City, right?"

"Uh, I think I remember," he said unconvincingly. "No, what are they again?"

Now that Gourry mentioned it, I realized I hadn't actually explained it to him at all.

"It's a person who was artificially created. They're made using human blood; their abilities are exactly the same as the person from whose blood they were formed."

Actually, clones, golems, homunculi, and various other magically made men were at first created using male bodily fluids, but new methods had been discovered in recent years. Many experiments had been performed with animal bones, distilling essences from different creatures and mixing them with human blood in various proportions.

Anyway, setting aside those strange cases for a moment, it was only important to note that a sorcerer could create with human blood an artificial human that was a hundred percent identical in appearance and abilities to the human who provided the source materials.

As just mentioned, homunculi vary in type and method of production. Although the sorcerers who develop new production methods could invent other names they find suitable. The prevailing sentiment of, "What's wrong with *homunculus?*" has ensured that most people still refer to them by the same name.

Complicating matters further, the products of older methods are called *smalls,* while those of newer experi-ments are called *copies.*

Copies, as the newer versions are called, are commonly used for human experiments and as guards (which has raised a number of human rights issues in recent times).

Though their appearance and abilities are no different from those of normal humans, the completed copy homunculus has no will or memory of its own and is otherwise indistinguishable from a flesh golem.

"So, if someone used my blood to create one of them, you'd get a soldier who could fight me to a draw?"

I shook my head.

"The basic abilities—strength, speed, reflexes—would certainly be the same. But homunculi wouldn't be able to match your skills at swordsmanship or with battle tactics. That is to say, even a duplicate with the same basic skill sets wouldn't have the same personality, movement patterns, or speech patterns. The homunculus doesn't have the benefit of experience, so there are limits. It's not the same as the original.

"Though, I suppose you *could* copy someone's speech patterns if you were familiar with them."

"So you mean that amateur we met last night might've created that Rezo?"

I nodded. It was a possibility worth considering.

"Look," I sighed. "We haven't had enough dealings with Rezo to tell if *that Rezo* was a man-made impostor or a close relative. And because the Vision sorcery was being relayed, I couldn't get a read on his aura, either."

"But you're pretty sure it's a fake?"

"Pretty sure. I mean, even if the real one is alive, it's not Rezo anymore!" I said, reminding Gourry of the transformation we'd both witnessed.

"Yeah," he agreed. It wasn't like you could just forget seeing something like that. "So what's your gut say?"

"Well, it's just a guess, but I think it's probably one of Rezo's minions using a facsimile of the Red Priest to send other minions to lure us to Sairaag. They probably want to avenge Rezo, and, failing that, drag our names through the mud."

It wasn't incredibly plausible, but it was the best guess I had.

"Hmm . . ." Gourry stared into space and rubbed his chin with his hand.

"What? You don't agree?"

"Hey, I'm allowed a differing opinion. Just because you thought of it doesn't make it *right!*" Gourry was getting snarky.

Oh, yeah? Well, what've you got, genius? Nothing? That's what I thought.

"Fine. But either way, the answer's in Sairaag."

"So I guess we're going to Sairaag," Gourry sighed.

"I guess we're going to Sairaag," I agreed.

Gourry turned toward the faint light of dawn on the horizon and a look of apprehension settled on his face.

***

"Glegh!"

That was the sound of Gourry's fist making hard contact with a man's solar plexus.

I cast my Elmekia Lance spell simultaneously, putting a different man down for the count.

That was the sixth group of would-be heroes we'd taken on that day.

"This is getting old," Gourry said, sounding like tedium personified. "Sixth team so far and it's not even noon . . . how many of these 'Allies of Justice' are we gonna have to fight before we get to Sairaag?"

"Maybe we should improve our disguise? Otherwise, we're not going to have any strength left by the time we get there."

"Sounds good, but before that . . . we've got more company." Gourry seemed as if he didn't know whether to spit or cry.

"Yeah, I know." I looked down the highway as I spoke.

The road twisted on a ways before disappearing behind a slightly elevated hill strewn with blue-colored stones. According to the last innkeeper we'd met, we would be able to see the next city once we reached it.

I noticed a small wooded area on the right-hand side of the highway, and some wheat fields. I also saw a row of mountain peaks beyond the hill in the distance.

As I was taking in the view, I detected what appeared to be a single black shadow on both sides of a tree?

No, it was a sorcerer in black clothes, his hood drawn down over his eyes.

"All right, come on out, whoever you are!" I called, as I walked on ahead with a swagger that was probably more accurately described as "an air of desperation."

"I owe you for last night," the sorcerer said. He had a young voice.

Eh?

Last night? Certainly we faced a sorcerer the night before, but he was alone . . .

"Surely you have not forgotten Vrumugun so soon?"

"Um, well . . ." I raised my eyebrows. Gourry, who was right beside me, did the same thing.

Of course I remembered Vrumugun. I remembered the previous night's encounter all too well. But this voice . . . well, he sounded different.

He came closer, and I was able to see his face. It was Vrumugun—definitely him, not just a resemblance.

Besides, who would want to impersonate someone with a name like Vrumugun? Anyway, how could he have followed us?

"I see," said Vrumugun, sounding disappointed with my answer.

"Jeez! You don't learn, do you, buddy? Surely *you* haven't forgotten how we whupped your butt?"

Vrumugun's face turned a little pink. "I have not. And today I have brought with me some assistance. Come forth!" he called.

I was going to ask Vrumugun if he knew the phrase "You and what army?" But just as I opened my mouth to speak, his "assistant" emerged from the trees.

"You—?!" I started and stopped, my jaw hanging open in surprise.

2 : THE LONG, LONG
: ROAD TO SAIRAAG

"**L**ong time no see, little girl," said the wolf-man to the pretty lady. What do you mean, *who?* Me! Don't you think I'm pretty? Or don't you think I'm a *lady?* No—better not answer that. Keep your mouth shut and nobody has to get hurt.

The wolf-man—or man-wolf, or were-dork, or whatever you want to call a guy who's half wolf, half troll and all ugly—was carrying a scimitar on his back and sneering in a familiar tone.

Oh, goody. And here I thought we'd never see each other again.

My long-lost pal's genetic profile broke down like this: he stood upright like a man, but had the head of a wolf and the regenerative powers of a troll. In fact, I'd once seen him heal from a sword wound right before my eyes. He also had the wit and intellect of a clump of mud, but I suppose that's neither here nor there.

"I see you're still all talk and no action, wolf-man," I jeered.

The wolf wilted.

Damn. That was easy.

"Don't you dare," Vrumugun began.

"Oh, I dare say I *do* dare. It's kind of what I do: I mean, I'm *daring* and so I dare—"

"Silence!" Vrumugun spat.

"Pssst," Gourry got my attention from behind. "Do you know that guy? Er, the dog . . . wolf . . . guy . . . thing?"

Typical.

"That's Dilgear, Gourry. Remember? *Dilgear.* He was part of our romp with Rezo and company?"

"Oh, yeah . . ." He craned his neck a little and squinted, then gave up. "Sorry. All dog-men look alike to me, I guess."

That's not terribly evolved of you, Gourry. Oh well. What was I going to do? Stop and give him a lecture on interspecies sensitivity? At any rate, Dilgear seemed to have recovered from the slight, and my attention shifted back to the matter before me. *Is there someone else there?*

I couldn't make out much of a face from the front, but it almost looked like . . .

Oh no.

Oh yes: the fish-man. And when I say "fish-man," I mean pretty much exactly what you think I mean: a fish . . . who is also a man.

Still having trouble with that idea? Okay, imagine a fish. Now, imagine a fish that's roughly the size of a human being. Now imagine that large fish having arms and legs that poke out of its fishy body. Got that much? Okay, you're done. That's a fish-man. Crazy, innit?

Fish-men are popular with city kids, who often collect small fish-man paintings and trade them with their fish-man-loving friends. These kids usually think it would be really cool to meet a fish-man . . . until they actually meet one. Then there's the screaming, and the crying and the nightmares. Fish-men are ugly business, people. That's all I'm saying.

Anyway, it was beginning to feel like some kind of warped animal farm.

"Don't tell me you're still hanging with this bunch of losers, Mister Nunsa," I tut-tutted.

The fish-man looked around as if he thought I might be talking to someone else. Finding no one, he returned his gaze to me. And he stared. Ever seen a fish stare? They're not big on blinking.

Knock it off, fish-man. That's creepy.

"Nunsa, you say?" the fish-man muttered at last.

Um . . . yeah?

It took me a minute, but I finally figured out what was going on: he wasn't Nunsa. I'd mistaken the fish-man in front of me for another pers—uh, fish-man.

I couldn't tell fish-men apart! So much for *my* inter-species sensitivity. On the upside, he didn't seem offended. On the contrary, he was flattered.

"You . . . you know that handsome and refined being they call *Nunsa?* You know Nunsa . . . p-p-personally?"

Handsome and refined?!

Okay, call me insensitive, but the fish-man I knew as Nunsa looked pretty much exactly like the one I was staring in the gills. And no offense, but I wouldn't call either one of them handsome. And nothing that smells like *that* could ever be considered *refined* as far as I'm concerned.

"I-I-I am flattered that you would even consider my modest physique in the same breath as one so handsome as N-Nunsa," the fish-man stammered.

Whoa, there, fishy. I'd prefer not to consider your physique any more than I have to.

"My name is Rahanim," the fish-man announced. "I will say to you but once, you would do well not to confuse us. Though Nunsa may be fair, I am—thanks to Lord Rezo— I am capable of swimming through the sky itself."

He didn't make a lot of sense, but he certainly seemed to enjoy the sound of his own voice. It wouldn't have made any difference to me, except that I knew we'd end up having to fight them in the end, and I would have preferred just getting on with it.

"Yeah, that's right!" Dilgear interrupted Rahanim. "And I'm stronger than I was the last time we met, so I'd appreciate a little respect, or else I'm gonna make you eat those words of yours—"

"Eat my fireball, chumps!" I'd had enough of the chitchat, so I sent a fireball hurtling toward the three motormouths.

That ought to get the party started.

Of course, I knew I wasn't going to take out all three in a single blow, but I figured I might start the thing out on the right foot, you know? Get things going in our favor?

"Hey! We weren't ready!" Vrumugun shouted out as he tumbled backward. Like I was supposed to warn them first.

This is a fight, you idiots.

Rahanim had gotten away. I spotted him in the middle of a wheat field. And Dilgear was . . . Where's Dilgear?

Oh, that's him over there. On fire. Nice shot!

"What do you think you're doing?!" the sorcerer screeched at the beast-man, whose smoking, barbecue-scented body had already stopped twitching.

I bet that hurt.

"Rahanim! Come!" Vrumugun called.

"Understood!" Rahanim shouted back, and as he did, he seemed to grow?

No, he wasn't growing—his feet had lifted off the ground. He was floating in midair!

Oh, he can swim through air. I get it.

The fish-man turned and, not a full second later he was back beside Vrumugun. The sorcerer pointed his right hand toward the belly of the loose-lipped fish-man. "Go," he ordered. "Slice them to ribbons."

By *them*, I think he meant *us*.

"As you wish," said the fish-man.

Rahanim sure didn't look fast enough to nail me and Gourry. Vrumugun had apparently underestimated our capabilities yet again.

Maybe that joker has some kind of death wish?

"Lina!" Gourry shouted just as I was feeling smug.

I looked around. Rahanim had vanished. Then a powerful gust of wind blew hard past my right flank.

"What the—?!" I lost my balance and fell sideways into the cornfield. I scrambled back up onto my feet as fast as I could—there was no way the great Lina Inverse was going to go out lying in a cornfield, cheeks against the grass, I'll tell you that much!

Damn. As I made my way back to a standing position, I saw that the shell-style guard over my right shoulder had been cleaved deep, and there was an ugly gash on the surface of the ruby talisman embedded there.

Damn, damn, damn. I love these shoulder guards.

"Hmph, I meant to cut off her head," Rahanim muttered, apparently not satisfied with the damage he'd done. He circled around, stalking me.

As soon as he'd started his attack, the fish-man's movements had gone from as slow as sludge to as fast as lightning. I'd completely lost track of him! Nothing moves that fast—certainly not a fish-man. I figured Vrumugun must have enveloped his body in a wind barrier. That was the only thing that would explain his sudden speed.

It seemed I'd been the one to underestimate my opponent that time. *Oops.*

"Did you catch that?" I asked Gourry, keeping my gaze in Rahanim's direction for caution's sake.

"Just the shadow," he replied, dejected.

I've said it before and I'll say it again: Gourry's swordsmanship is absolutely, hands-down, no-question-about-it top rate. If Rahanim was moving so fast that Gourry couldn't track him . . .

This is not good.

In a large open space like that, an indiscriminate attack spell wasn't our only option, but it was probably the one most likely to succeed. Except for the fact that we couldn't be sure of who else might be hit in the fray.

That leaves only one other option . . .

Rahanim's form vanished again with a *whoosh.*

"Daa!" Gourry and I both cried out as we ducked.

. . . running for our lives!

A gust of wind tore over my head. Rahanim wasn't able to maneuver very tightly at that flight speed, and we weren't able to keep up with his movements well enough to manage any kind of counter. All he could do was charge head-on, and all we could do was . . . duck.

It was pretty sad, as battles go.

"Hold still," Rahanim muttered as he circled around again.

If I didn't think of something, we were going to do that same dance over and over until one of us forgot to duck or fish-face got tired. So I thought of something.

I began casting a spell.

"Foolish girl! Do you really think you'll be able to hit me?" As he finished speaking, his form vanished once more.

Nope. Foolish fish, do you really think I need to?

I finished chanting at the same moment he disappeared. An instant later, he charged straight at me through the middle of the wheat field.

VWOMP! A powerful shockwave came with the sound. I planted my feet, but I was still knocked back several yards. Even so, the wind barrier I had placed around my body deflected his, disorienting Mr. Fish-face and protecting me from any real damage.

Now's my chance!

As the fish-man struggled for balance, I began chanting my next spell. Rahanim turned and headed toward Gourry.

Gourry answered with a flash of silver!

All Gourry's sword managed to do was mow down a few stalks of wheat, but he must have made Rahanim dizzy somehow, as the fish-man spun around weakly and floated higher into the sky. He swam around in circles for a minute, focusing on something in the distance. Then, just as suddenly, the atmosphere changed and he returned his gaze to Gourry and me.

Whatever he was up to, he'd given me enough time to complete my next spell.

"Bram Gush!" I shouted, forcefully launching my arrow of condensed wind energy. Though its effect varied from target to target, if my arrow hit its mark, it had enough power to pulverize a brick wall.

It flew straight and true toward the high ground to the spot where Vrumugun had been, and . . . *direct hit!*

I'll—uh—leave out the details in deference to those of you who may want to eat something sometime in the near future. Or, you know, ever again. *Yeech.* Let's just say it was nasty and leave it at that.

"Sir Vrumugun!" Rahanim called out in a panic.

I cast my next spell while he was distracted. "Ray Wing!" I said, and the winds lifted me into the air with a whoosh.

Ray Wing is a spell that wraps a wind barrier around the one who casts it, enabling him or her for high-speed flight. Though it's harder to control than Levitation, you can't beat it for velocity. With Ray Wing on your side, you could easily beat a bird in a race.

"Gourry! Grab on!" I loosened the barrier for a moment.

"What are we doing?!" Gourry asked as I whisked him up from the middle of the wheat field.

"We're running away!"

"Damn you!" Rahanim barked.

Ever heard a fish-man bark? It's kind of weird. Anyway . . .

Eager for revenge, he lunged for the two of us.

"Ugh!" *That stung.*

Even without Vrumalungadingdong, the fish-man was moving unbelievably fast. The sorcerer's spell must have been the kind with a fixed duration—one that could survive beyond the jerk who cast it. It wouldn't be hard to beat fish-face once his flight spell collapsed, but since we had no idea how long that was gonna take, it seemed stupid to dance around and wait.

We hightailed it over the summit of the next hill and—just like the old innkeeper promised—we could make out a town just ahead.

Rahanim revved up and rammed the two of us again.

This is getting old.

"Well, we're not getting away!" Gourry shouted, glomming onto my hips in a pose that would have made me blush if I'd thought about it at the time.

Ray Wing's speed is proportional to the weight being carried and the magical capacity of the one casting the spell. With Gourry holding onto me, we couldn't move fast enough to shake the fish-man off.

If we can just get to town!

"Gourry, I've got it!" I said. "We're gonna use disguises. The fish-man'll probably say something to us. When he does, keep your answers short, and absolutely do NOT call me by my real name! Talk as little as possible, got it?"

"That's your plan—don't talk?"

"Don't talk, do *not* draw your sword—and *try* to keep your temper in check! Got it?!"

Gourry didn't answer.

Could it be that sometimes he doubts my genius? Nah . . . that's just silly.

***

We passed through the town gates so fast we blew over an old woman selling fruits and vegetables near the entrance.

Oranges hit the street like marbles, and pedestrians flew every which way like chickens in a bar fight.

I have no idea what that means either. Just go with it.

"Hey, hey, hey! Lina!"

"Gourry, you can file a complaint later!" We shot down the main thoroughfare, my eyes searching right and left . . .

That's the spot, right there!

We threw on the brakes and rammed Rahanim smashing him through several stalls. Without stopping, I doubled us back down the alley, and there I canceled Ray Wing.

We were in a lumberyard. There were boards, lengths of squared timber, and freshly cut trees piled up on the ground and against a stone wall.

"Gourry! Put everything but our armor on top of the lumber! And don't forget what I told you earlier! There's no time to explain, just do it—fast!" As I spoke, I removed my shoulder guards and mantle, took my short sword off, and peeled down both gloves. I put my mantle on Gourry and hid the rest—along with Gourry's armor—on the other side of the lumber. Finally, I stuffed my bandanna into my trouser pocket and sat down calmly next to Gourry.

"Don't talk more than you have to," I reminded him. I was stilling my mind when . . .

Rahanim's form appeared at the opening of the alley. The fish-man paused, then said, "Nowhere to run," in a flat tone.

"I'm sorry . . . what?" I gazed up at him and acted like I had absolutely no idea what he meant. I'm not a bad little actress, if I do say so myself.

Just as I predicted, Rahanim got quiet and thought for a while.

"It is useless to try and deceive me, Lina Inverse!" he said at last.

I blinked. "Lina who?"

Fish-face, nervous and fidgety, looked around the area.

"It seems there's been a mistake," he sighed. "Have a sorceress with red hair and a swordsman with yellow hair passed by here recently?"

"Um . . . Leon, maybe it was them?" I said to Gourry.

"Eh? Huh?!" Gourry was caught totally off-guard.

"You saw them?!" Rahanim spoke again before Gourry could overcome his stupidity.

"Oh, yeah," I said. "Right before our eyes, whoosh— two of 'em, right? They flew that way." I pointed to the other end of the alley. "I think they went . . . about two blocks down . . . and turned . . . left."

"Pardon me." With that, Rahanim sped down the alley in the direction I'd pointed.

Hee hee hee hee! I broke into giggles. *Success!*

"Um, what happened just now?" Gourry asked, a puzzled look on his face. The fish-man was good and gone.

"He can't do individual differentiation," I replied.

"He can't . . . individual . . . what?"

"Remember back at the hill, when you saw Dilgear and you said you couldn't tell dog-men apart? Well, it's the same with him—he can't really tell humans apart. That's why we ducked into the alley, so he'd lose sight of us for a minute. Our hair color was the same, and he'd seen us head in here, but our clothes were different. And it didn't make sense to him that we could just be sitting here calmly. That's why he said 'Nowhere to run'—because he wasn't sure it was us!" I explained. "And since he couldn't be sure, that's why he believed me."

"Huh . . ." Gourry scratched his chin, looking like he couldn't quite accept it just yet.

"Is it really that hard?" he asked. "I mean, I can tell two cat breeds apart pretty easily."

"Well, sure—that's because they're different breeds," I clarified. "The sizes, patterns, colors, and shapes are all different. That's completely different than telling two cats of the *same* breed apart. Right?"

"Well, yeah."

"Werewolves can actually tell us apart by our scents, though—"

"Shh!" Gourry interrupted. The reason was immediately apparent: a shadow had appeared at the end of the alley. An intriguingly fish-shaped shadow.

Rahanim?! Maybe he figured it out. No, wait . . .

"Hey!" the fish-man called out in my direction. "Are you sure it was two down and to the left?"

Nope, he hadn't caught on.

"Hmm, well, now that you mention it, I'm not sure. It might have been three down," I lied shamelessly.

"I see, then. Pardon me." The fish-man vanished down the alleyway once more.

"See?" I grinned and giggled as we watched him go.

***

"Man, sorcerers must get really gloomy having to wear mantles like this all the time," Gourry mumbled while digging into his meal.

"Oh, quit your moaning. If it beats risking your life in an unnecessary battle, then it's a small sacrifice, isn't it?" I glared.

After managing to shake Rahanim, Gourry and I had visited the local tailor to complete our disguises.

I was wearing the white robes of a priestess. I'd tied my hair back in a ponytail, and I had my bandanna on as usual. I'd thrown away the beloved shoulder guards that Rahanim had cut, and my mantle and gloves were stuffed into a knapsack. My short sword was fastened behind me. No observer would have been able to spot it underneath my priestess mantle.

Gourry had put a large mantle on over his iron serpent breastplate. He wore a circlet and a pendant talisman that had little jingly things hanging here and there. He looked like a sorcerer, except . . . well, his hairstyle was somewhat conservative for a sorcerer, and the bulge from the sword at his hip was visible under his robe.

Also, he had a look on his face that shouted *I am in misery.*

What a crybaby! Like sorcery is a fate worse than death!

I'd ended up a sorceress because I was too weak to make my way with a sword, and my temperament wasn't exactly suited to a life of pacifism, and anyway, neither of those roles appealed to me at all.

"I know, but still," Gourry muttered gloomily, hunched under his mantle. "These are *costumes*, not disguises! Anyone could tell."

"No, it would depend on who was doing the looking." I sipped a bit of soda as I spoke. "Look, all those 'heroes' have spotted us because we looked *exactly* like those nasty-looking wanted posters. After a change of clothes and hairstyle, there's no way they could pick us out from just our portraits. Complete strangers—bounty hunters, for instance—would not recognize us." I smiled and stuck my chest out confidently as I spoke. That was when a man's voice called out to me.

"Hey, hey, little Lina! Yer chipper as usual, eh?"

My eyes narrowed.

The voice was coming from a mercenary standing right behind me.

He didn't seem to bear me any ill intent.

He was the same age as Gourry, or maybe a little younger. He had flaming red hair and an attractive face, but he wore a goatee that was completely wrong for his age, undercutting anything positive he had going for him in the looks department.

Of course, I'm sure he would disagree.

"Hey," Gourry said with a small wave. "How've you been?"

"Oh, about the same," the man replied, waving back.

What the—?

I was the only one out of the loop. Don't you hate when that happens?

I leaned over the table and whispered to Gourry in a small voice, "Who is that?"

"What do you mean? It's Lantz . . . ain't it?"

"Lantz?!" I swung my head back again and took another long, hard look at his face. "How about that? His beard's longer."

Gourry and I knew Lantz, another traveling mercenary, from our recent adventures in Atlas City. He was one hell of a swordsman—certainly first rate, if not the absolute cream of the crop. I didn't recognize him at first because of the beard.

What a bad idea *that* was.

"The beard throw ya? Yeah, I figured I'd just let it grow while I was moaning and groaning and healing in bed. Figured I could use a different look anyway."

"Were you shooting for ugly? Or did you just find it by accident?" I wondered aloud.

"Heh. Like you're ones to talk . . ." Lantz chuckled.

What? Why that—! There's no common decency at all anymore, I tell you!

I sat back in my seat at the table and focused on the meal, biting my tongue both literally and figuratively.

"Ouch!"

Sensing my glare as he stuffed his mouth full of food, he spoke: "Ah, I'm just kidding. I mean, that outfit shows off alotta bosom improvement. Can't argue with that."

Oh, swell. That's just what a gal wants to hear, isn't it? I guess that Lantz is a pretty good guy after all . . . riiiiiight.

Grrr . . .

I raised my hand before I raised my voice. "Madam, two servings of the first appetizer you have listed here, please!" I shouted.

"Tell us the truth, cutie girl," Lantz leaned in and dropped his voice to a whisper. "Are you a demon?"

I seethed in Lantz's direction.

Seethe, seethe, seethe.

"My, oh my. Poor big bro. He ought to get a medal for spending *every day* with you."

Lantz had been so impressed by Gourry's swordsmanship that he'd taken to calling him "big bro" as a sign of respect. The names he called me were less adoring.

"Eh, it's not so bad," Gourry piped up in my defense. "I mean, sure, she eats a lot. And, yeah, she's always getting us into trouble. She's got a nasty mouth, sure, and she's not exactly hot—"

"What?! You *totally* eat more than I do! Don't you just sit there and nod your head with him!" I snapped.

"Okay, okay, calm down," Gourry cooed. "Let's just forget about all that for a minute. Lantz, can I ask you something?"

"What's up?"

"When you saw us, you recognized us right away, didn't you? I mean, not that we're—uh—*in disguise* or anything."

Lantz took a deep breath, held it, then exhaled slowly, as if he wasn't quite sure how to word his answer. I like to think it was because he was afraid of offending me, but that probably wasn't it.

"Big bro," he said, "I don't mean you any disrespect, but . . . those aren't *disguises*, they're more like *costumes*. I knew you right off."

"I see," Gourry turned and glared at me as if to say *I told you so.*

Oh, so what? You're going to take his word over mine, you big bum?

"Well, what if—what if you didn't know us personally, huh? I mean, what if you were just trying to recognize us from a—uh—a portrait, say? Would you know us then?" I asked, hastening to add, "Hypothetically, of course."

Lantz laughed and leaned in close, "When you say *portrait*, you wouldn't be referring to a wanted poster by any chance, would you?"

"You?!" I stopped and lowered my voice. "You've seen them?"

"Well, yeah." Lantz chuckled. "Do you know what kind of price you two have got on your heads? I can't go two steps without someone talking about it. Everybody wants to know what you did to earn it. I mean, *I* know it must be some kind of mistake, but most folks figure you two for pure evil.

"So, what happened? What did you do that pissed off that big shot enough to earn yourselves a king's bounty?"

Who, us? Oh, nothing special. We saved the world and stymied the Source of All Chaos. That's all.

"Um . . . this and that," I said.

"So you're trying to dodge the guy who put up the bounty, huh?"

"No, we're accepting his invitation to Sairaag, actually," Gourry volunteered.

Ix-nay on the etails-day, Gourry! Lantz doesn't need to know our business!

81

"Counterattack, eh? Makes sense," Lantz nodded. "So, big bro, what do you say I go with you to Sairaag, huh? I mean, with all due respect to your disguise, I don't think it's gonna keep bounty hunters off your tail. What do you say?"

I have to admit it: that wasn't what I expected to hear from dear ol' Lantz. The last time we'd had occasion to work with him, he'd turned and run as soon as he'd found out there were demons involved.

"Now hang on just a second," I interjected before Gourry had a chance to say something stupid. "It's real easy for you to volunteer, but whoever ends up being on the other end of our fight—and we don't know all the facts yet—but whoever that ends up being, it's not going to be easy."

"I understand that. Goes without saying, even," Lantz answered, at ease. "Listen, I owe you guys, but I'm not promising I'll fight this guy with you. I just . . . I was planning on going to Sairaag anyway. See?"

"Going to Sairaag? You're not coming from there?" I asked, perplexed. Lantz told us he was going to Sairaag when he left Atlas City, which was more than a week before we'd left. I'd figured he'd already done his business there and was headed the other way.

"What happened?" Gourry asked.

Lantz's face took on an awkward expression. "Well, a bunch of things . . ."

Ha ha ha ha ha ha ha ha! A girl!

Ah well, anyway.

"You're sure you want to do this? The guy we're up against this time is a lot tougher than the last one," I explained.

Lantz was dumbstruck for a minute. *Typical.*

"Well," he sighed. "I'll just have to get out of there before I start slowing you guys down, I guess."

"If that's what you wanna do, it's fine by me," I said, looking him right in the eye. "But I'm not going to sugarcoat it: when the time comes, you'd better run hard and fast. This time, we can't guarantee that anyone who follows us *in* is getting *out* in one piece."

His face red and serious, Lantz swallowed forcibly and nodded.

***

The weather the next morning was nothing short of beautiful. The path we were on made the hiking easy, and at that pace, we expected to arrive in Sairaag by noon.

Silly or not, our disguises and fake names seemed to be working. Since our makeovers, the bounty hunters—or Allies of Justice (or whatever it was they wanted to call themselves)—and Rezo's minions had both gone missing. Well, I wouldn't say I missed them, exactly, but you know what I mean.

"Looks like we're gonna get there safe and sound," said Lantz in a voice so annoyingly cheerful it might have qualified as chipper.

"Well, we're not there yet. Let's not get careless," I reminded him.

"Righty-o," Lantz chirped.

Righty-o?!

"We've got to make it through that forest first," Gourry pointed. "They call it the Miasma Forest. There's some kind of strange presence that hangs over it, making it impossible to sense enemies once you're inside. If anyone's going to attack us, they'll do it in there."

Lantz and I both stopped and took in the sight up ahead. Then something occurred to me . . .

"Gourry, how did you know that? I mean, about the forest being called the Miasma Forest and all."

I knew the legend of the forest well. The tale centers around a swordsman who used the Sword of Light to slay the demon beast Zanaffar and avenge the destruction of old Sairaag. The demon was said to have bled so much that the forest was completely submerged in a lake of blood until the great beast finally expired. The lake eventually receded, but ever since, a strange presence has hung over the woods. Whether it was because of that legend or because of the many crimes committed in the woods since, the Miasma Forest's infamy was several times greater than that of the slums of the port city of Froueib.

Froueib—as I'm sure you know—is not exactly the kind of place you go looking for tea and crumpets, you know what I'm saying?

The legend of the Miasma Forest was well known among sorcerers, but Gourry didn't even know where he was half the time. Sure, he's a descendant of the Swordsman of Light, but still, I didn't figure him for being too up on local legends.

"I—uh—I stopped by here once a while back." The look on his face clearly said, *I don't wanna talk about it.*

"Uh huh," Lantz said.

"You don't say," I added. Neither Lantz nor I was very good at taking a hint. We both stared at Gourry.

"Wh-what? What are you staring at me for?!" Gourry stammered.

"Come to think of it, you didn't look too thrilled when we decided to come to Sairaag," I mused.

"Aw, you dog!" Lantz exclaimed. "I bet there's a string of broken hearts in town with your name on each and every one—am I right?

"Oh! Maybe there's a whole bunch of little Gourrys running around town swinging toy swords at shadows, huh?" he added.

"I bet you're right," I chimed in. " 'Papa came to see us!' one group will say, and then another gaggle will appear: 'No, that's *our* papa!' "

"Yeah, and then they'll fight! Multiple armies of diminutive blonds!" Lantz guffawed.

I was honestly surprised Lantz even knew the word *diminutive*. Not bad.

"You two," Gourry sighed.

Lantz and I both smiled.

***

The Miasma Forest could easily have been renamed the Quiet Forest. The Silent Forest, maybe? I don't know. Whichever one has a better ring to it. My point being, there was none of your regular forest sounds in those trees. Oh, it smelled right; a raw green scent hung in the air—like the essence of freshness itself—and the breeze was cool too, but the trees . . . the trees were thick, and their trunks were as black as gloom.

"Creepy," Lantz observed, his body quivering a bit.

"Yep . . . and odd," I added, referring to the strange presence we all sensed.

The place certainly deserved its name; an odd presence hung throughout the whole of the forest. The quiet . . . it was the quiet that got to you. You'd expect to hear a bird call or an insect buzz, but there was none of that. Even the twigs that snapped under our feet seemed too afraid to make a sound. It was as if the place was something out of a dream. The whole forest was dead, except for that presence. We could feel it hovering over us in the treetops, watching from thickets, and waiting in the underbrush. The presence was embodied by the forest itself.

"It's just like the legend," I said, more to hear my own voice than for any other reason. "The presence is so strong it numbs your senses. It would be impossible to feel an enemy lying in wait."

Right on cue, there was a rustling in a nearby thicket.

"What was that?!" Gourry jumped.

"There!" Lantz pointed. They both drew their swords.

Fearing an enemy decoy, I spun around and turned my attention to the opposite direction. If we knew for sure there were varmints in them woods, I could pound them with an indiscriminate attack spell and not have a second thought about it. But, what if there were innocent people out there? What if someone just got lost?

The thicket was still.

So were we.

"What now?" Gourry whispered at last.

"For all we know, that could've been a rabbit," Lantz said, and he was right. Because of the presence, I couldn't even tell if that sound had been made by a human.

Well, we can't just stand here staring forever.

"Ummrr . . . ummh . . ." The sound continued.

"Shhh! Did you hear that?" I whispered.

"Rrmm . . ." There was a faint moaning coming from the direction of the thicket. The voice was young . . . and female.

"Hey, it's a *girl*." Lantz perked up immediately and headed into the bramble.

"H-hey, Lantz!" Gourry called out worriedly.

But Lantz was already in the thick of it by that time. Sadly, it's a man's nature to forget that women can be dangerous.

"It's okay," Lantz responded. "She's all right—she just fainted."

Gourry and I looked at each other and shook our heads for a moment before following Lantz into the thicket. There we found a young woman, lying prone.

Actually, it would have been more accurate to call her a *girl*. She couldn't have been much older than me, if she was older at all. She wore a short-sleeved tunic with—uh—hotpants. She had long gloves on both arms and soft socks. She had brown hair, cut short and wrapped in a bright red bandanna. A large knife hung from her hip.

She looked something like a female bandit-in-training. The boyish costume actually suited her; I mean, I wouldn't have picked it out, but you know, it was cute. Still, she must've been chilly, what with her midriff exposed like that.

Are her boobs bigger than mine? Dammit!

The three of us stood a short distance away and stared down at the girl.

"What do we now?" Gourry asked.

"Well, if you gotta ask, big bro, better let me go first. Heh heh . . ."

"Ew! We don't have time for pervert jokes!" I snapped at Lantz. "For all we know this might be a trap, but just in case it's not, well, we can't just leave her like this."

"So, we'll help her out. Cute girls can't be bad guys, you know. That wouldn't make any sense." He kept staring at her.

Lantz, you're an idiot.

"Makes sense to me," Gourry joined in the idiot choir.

Et tu, Gourry? Et tu?

"Hey, how you doing there, miss? You want to tell us what the heck happened?" Lantz made small talk with the girl while helping her to her feet. Her movements were slow and labored; she seemed confused, like maybe she'd taken a blow to the head.

At least they have something in common.

"Uh . . . mmm . . . ah . . . urm . . ." The girl moaned repeatedly. When she finally opened her eyes, she did so like a kitten seeing the world for the first time. She was pretty oblivious.

"Mm . . . huh?" she said, first staring Lantz in the face, then having a look around.

Finally, she snapped her fingers.

"He got me," she murmured. "Damn that Zelgadiss!"

"Zelgadiss?!" Gourry and I exclaimed together.

"You know Zel?" I asked.

"Of course I know him, I—aaaaaaah?! Lina Inverse?! Wh-wha—?" She went all inarticulate and started rummaging around in her hotpants' pockets, fishing something out.

It was a wanted poster. She held it up and looked back and forth from it to us, and from us to it and so on. "I knew it!" she shrieked. "Lina Inverse and Gourry Gabriev! Lina Inverse and Gourry Gabriev!

"And some nobody!" she added at last.

"Hey!" Lantz blurted out, scowling.

I think you hurt his widdle feelings.

"I'm sorry, miss," I said, smiling through gritted teeth. "But I'm afraid you have us confused with those scoundrels. Don't feel bad—it's a common mistake, but we have absolutely nothing to do with *those* people." I can lie shamelessly.

Too bad she didn't buy it. She held the poster in her left hand and pointed at us with her right, shouting, "Nuh-uh! There's no mistake! You might be able to fool amateurs with that crap, but I, Eris, a bounty hunter of world renown, cannot be so easily deceived!"

"World renown? I've never heard of any Eris the Bounty Hunter." I looked to Lantz.

"Me neither," he said, turning to Gourry.

"Nope," Gourry shrugged.

"W-well, I will be world-renowned! This capture will put me on the map—Ha HA! How lucky is this, huh?!" she said, drawing her knife with her right hand and springing toward me. "I advise you it's best if you come quietly."

Oh yeah, right. In your dreams, toots.

I grabbed her wrist and twisted it up hard.

"Owwww! Ow! Ow! Ow! H-hey! Let me go, you horrible woman!" the soon-to-be-world-renowned bounty hunter Eris exclaimed, struggling weakly against my grip.

"What?! You drew a knife and jumped *me!* And I'm a horrible woman?!"

"The one who's losing gets to say who's horrible!" she yelped.

Can't argue with logic like that.

"Birds of a feather, huh?" Lantz laughed.

"LANTZ! Don't you *even*—! And GOURRY, if you think I can't see you smiling over there, you're sadly mistaken! Now Eris—" I paused to take a breath—"there are a few things I'd like you to explain."

"I'd rather die than talk to wanted criminals," Eris spat, adding a short shrill laugh as punctuation.

"That can be arranged," I promised.

"Hey, whoa now, let's just back that wagon up," she chortled. "I was *kidding!* C'mon! What would you like to know?"

So, she's not an idiot. Noted.

"What do you know about Zelgadiss?" I asked, not letting go of her delicate wrist.

"Well, I've been after his head since the wanted poster came out—hey, that hurts! He got to Sairaag about five days ago, and he's been trying to find the Red Priest ever since. I guess he wants to talk about the bounty."

"Hold on! So Rezo the Red Priest is already in Sairaag?!" I asked, interrupting her in mid-sentence. She looked at me like I was retarded.

"Of course he is," she sighed. Then, like she'd just tasted something awful she asked, "Don't tell me you came here to kill Lord Rezo, too?!"

I could tell from the tone in her voice that she, like the rest of the world, was completely fooled by the Red Priest's ruse and, like them, she considered him a living saint. Which of course meant that she saw us as potential saint-killers. If I cared what she thought one way or the other, I might have been upset about that. But I didn't, so I wasn't. Anyway, there wasn't time to explain the whole thing—and it wasn't like she would have believed us anyway. So I took a different approach.

"Look, you have it all wrong. Those wanted posters are the result of someone framing us and misleading the Red Priest. It's all a big, goofy misunderstanding, got it? We came to Sairaag to straighten things out. That's all. I know you're not going to believe me, but there you have it."

Lies, lies, lies . . . Girl, I'm good at this.

"Anyway, Zelgadiss split off from us awhile ago, and we have no idea what he's up to. He may be after the Red Priest too, all the more reason that we should talk to him. So . . . please, tell us what the situation is in Sairaag right now."

"Well." She scratched her head with her free hand and then decided to talk. "Okay, but I'm not really sure what you want to know."

"Everything."

"The Red Priest arrived in Sairaag about a month ago. Pretty soon it was going around the whole region that he was staying with the high priest and that they were looking for the three of you. Then the wanted posters came out and, well, next I guess I spotted Zelgadiss—in an area just outside of the city, and I followed him here."

She continued. "Zelgadiss is traveling with the high priest's daughter, and they tried to take the Red Priest's life."

"Hold on!" I stopped her again. "Zel, I can understand. But why would the high priest's daughter want to kill the Red Priest?"

Eris shrugged her shoulders. "How am I supposed to know? Anyway, they didn't manage to kill him, but the city's in a huge uproar over the whole thing."

"That figures," I said.

Dammit, Zelgadiss.

I promised myself I'd give him an earful when next we met.

"Of course, there was no place they could hide in the city, so I followed them here, into the Miasma Forest," Eris explained.

"You came after them all by yourself?" I asked incredulously. "Why didn't you call someone for help?"

"And split the reward? Do I look like an idiot to you? Anyway, I figured I had a better chance of going unnoticed if I were alone. But apparently they noticed me anyway . . . I got ambushed, see."

"Guess that plan worked out for you, then." I chuckled.

What a hardhead.

"Oh, shut up." Eris was not amused.

"Well, I think we got the gist of it, anyway. So, now we need to figure out our plan from here . . . right, Gourry?"

"Yeah?" Gourry looked at me like he had no idea what I'd just said. "Oh, sorry, was I supposed to be listening?"

"You . . . aa . . . aah . . . ?!" I lost it. "YES! Yes, you were supposed to be listening. Do we have your attention now?"

Gourry nodded his head.

"Good! Okay, Zelgadiss is somewhere in this forest—should I say that again slowly or do you understand?!"

"Got it: Zelgadiss is here," Gourry repeated cheerfully. "So why don't we go look for him?"

Why don't we?!

"How exactly are we supposed to do that?" I wondered.

"Hmm. I didn't think about that part much."

"You don't think much AT ALL do you, Gourry?!" I could feel my frustration maxing out.

Breathe . . . breathe . . .

"Getting all red-faced like that can't be good for you, Lina," Gourry said, sounding genuinely concerned.

Lantz watched our little give-and-take with awe. "You two should take that act on the road," he said, laughing.

awhile," Gourry answered. "Wish it had been

ku's only brow twitched. "Well, now. This is
d." His half-lips turned upward, forming a
rtainly has been awhile."

d on my cuff a couple of times.

asked without turning.

ay . . . *Mazoku* just now?" she asked me in a

et a lesser demon one time and he didn't
all like *that*." Eris was horrified.

a higher-ranking variety," I explained.

ach higher-ranking?"

fference between a tiger and a house cat."

ris shrieked as she took off running.

tention of stopping her. It was better that
re was no chance we could fight him and
the same time.

s let out a weird yelp from somewhere
d and looked.

r loomed before her, blocking her escape path.

We are *on the road, smartass.*

"All right, here is the plan," I announced. "Before we head into town, we find Zel and we figure out exactly who we're dealing with here. First Zel. Then Sairaag. Got it?"

Gourry and Lantz both nodded.

"Oh, wait! What do we do about her?" Lantz said, indicating Eris.

"Me? Ah . . . er . . . well . . . heh . . ." Eris began laughing nervously. "I think I should probably be going now."

You're not going anywhere.

"If we let her run off, she could set the whole city on us," I reasoned. "If we take her with us, she'll slow us down. But since she's not our enemy, it's not like we can just kill her . . . can we?"

"No, but we could knock her out and leave her here," Lantz suggested.

"That sounds like our best—" Gourry chimed in.

"H-hold on a second!" Eris cried. "No *way* am I just going to stand here and let you knock me out. Not that I . . . I mean . . . Well, first of all, I . . ."

Before she could finish stammering, the thicket rustled.

Everyone jumped for cover. Gourry and Lantz each dove to the side, and just as they did, a white spear shot through the gap between them. I let Eris' hand go and scrambled back to my feet. The men had already drawn their swords. Gourry discarded the black mantle from his disguise.

"Hmm . . . warriors with limber bodies I see." The voice was coming from the silhouette of a man somewhere behind the swaying thicket.

Eris trembled silently for a moment then squeaked, "Wh-what *is* that?"

Her reaction wasn't all that surprising, considering . . .

The silhouette was clearly that of a man in a state of extreme physical fitness. As he moved closer, we could make out the fact that he was dressed all in black and that his face—the left side, anyway—was comely, if a little frigid.

On the other side, though—the right side—his face . . . was missing. There was nothing there: no brow, no hair, no eye, no ear. No nothing.

Everything to the right of the center of his face—his nose, lips and everything else—just . . . vanished. There was naught but a mass of smooth, pale flesh.

"Mazoku," I explained in a small voice, intoning the word with the respect it deserved.

"I am Vizea, a servant to Lord Rezo," it said. "It is a pleasure to make your acquaintance."

"Going someplace, little girl?" The spider licked at its lips as it spoke.

A giant spider. Of course. What did you expect?

It had eight legs and an enormous spidery abdomen. In every respect it was exactly how you would envision a giant spider to be, except . . . its flesh and head were human.

I'll skip the rest of the anatomical details, figuring you'd probably lose your lunch.

All that mattered to me was, given its hybrid nature: could it spin a web? If it *could*, well, that would make things more difficult.

"Let her go, Baaz," a different voice called out. "She's no threat. You can toy with random humans in your spare time."

The third voice emanated from a sorcerer clad in black robes. Though his face and his wardrobe were unremarkable, there was a ruby embedded in his forehead that, for some reason, drew my attention.

"Hmph," the man-spider spat. "As you wish, Vrumugun."

"What?!" Gourry and I shouted in unison.

The sorcerer smiled and laughed. "This time," he said, "victory will be mine."

"Wait just a minute, you!" I objected. "You can't be Vrumugun! Vrumugun's dead!"

"Oh, come now," the sorcerer chuckled. "You didn't really think your attack would be sufficient to kill me, did you?"

S-sufficient? Well, yeah, I did, actually . . .

The day that he and Rahanim and Dilgear attacked us . . . well, I *know* my spell hit him squarely. Gourry and I had seen the results with our own eyes! I didn't care if he was a dragon, a troll, or a cockroach—there was no way anyone could have survived that hit!

"Wow! He's still alive. Pretty defiant little guy, huh?" Gourry asked in a half-admiring tone.

Defiant wasn't the word I would've used, but it would do.

"Well, I guess now it's three-on-three, huh?" I made an effort to laugh boldly while Eris was frozen under the stare of the spider-guy.

"No, I'm sorry . . . but, no." Vrumugun smiled silently, wagging a finger that pointed overhead.

A dancing shadow was weaving its way through the sunlight filtering through the tree branches.

Rahanim!

I glanced sideways at Eris. "It now looks like it's four-on-four, then."

"Hey! No way! Don't count *me* in on this!" Eris protested.

"Oh, but it seems you are still at a disadvantage," a low voice called out.

. . . *Oh, come ON. Another one?*

A creature materialized behind Vizea. He had rough hair, a stocky build, and he looked like the ugly love child of a troll and a blow demon. He might have been a chimera of some sort.

"Wouldn't you agree, Mr. Vizea?" it said.

"Oh, yes. Quite." As the Mazoku spoke, he raised his right hand high into the air and snapped his fingers.

The miasma in the forest thickened . . . rustling . . . the trees almost seemed to close in around us. Then . . .

"Eeek!" Eris cried out in a shrill voice. Gourry and Lantz froze, and a chill ran down my spine.

One by one, the lesser demons emerged from within the woods. They numbered close to a dozen.

It made sense if you thought about it: whether an impostor or the real McCoy, Rezo was in Sairaag. Of course he would have that kind of force at his disposal. He'd probably heard that Zelgadiss had fled into the woods and sent troops. Then Vrumugun, who had somehow survived our last encounter, stumbled into the scene by chance . . . and voilá! There we were, surrounded.

I hadn't wanted to believe that the sorcerer had survived, but, he had the fish-man by his side, and, unlike Rahanim, he could recognize us at a glance.

It certainly was the most logical possibility.

In which case, our disguises might not have been effective after all.

Of course, the possibility also existed that *Vrumugun* was some sort of family name and that this guy was only familiar with "Lina" and "Gourry" from a secondhand source.

Then again, none of that really mattered. The only pressing concern was how to beat him—whoever he was—in the here and now. And it might have seemed possible, were it not for the lesser demons closing in on us. If it hadn't been for them, we could have broken out of the encirclement and made a run for it.

Brief interjection: Lesser demons are the lowest rank of the order of beings known as Mazoku. Just the same, normal warriors and sorcerers are no match for them. Earth, fire, water, and wind shamanic spells have little effect on them, and while physical attacks are effective in *theory*, their hides are tougher than dragon scales.

Though of course they were no match for me, the most brilliant and gifted sorceress of my era—the problem was that there were just too darn many of them!

"Where are my manners?" the troll-demon said as he turned to face us directly. "I haven't introduced myself yet."

Oh, goody. Like I don't have enough problems? Now I have to keep demon names straight.

Behind us, Baaz the man-spider moved silently sideways.

"My name in your human language is *Goluas*," the demon volunteered. "My true name is . . ."

He opened his mouth wide and let out a deafening roar. The treetops swayed violently, scattering green leaves everywhere. The fierce shockwave shook our bones.

Our screams were drowned out by the demon's bellow. Though our injuries weren't serious, the aural attack had been enough to knock us flat on our backs. We were stunned.

Before we had time to recover our senses, a bevy of white spears rained down around us! The missiles had sprung forth from the flesh on the right side of Vizea's face.

We were at war.

★★★

"Eeee!" Eris produced a pitiful, high-pitched wail as she dodged the pale projectiles. The flesh spears stuck into the spot right beside her and quivered. Gourry parried the spears coming at him while they were still high in the air. Lantz cut things a little closer.

I leapt backward over Eris and in the direction of Baaz the man-spider. I drew my sword and slashed at him while starting to chant a spell under my breath.

"Ha-HAH!" The man-spider quite nearly giggled with delight as he leapt up onto a nearby tree trunk. His head pointed down and his belly up. His positioning was poor. I took advantage of the chance to retreat.

"Gaah!" Baaz leapt for me. Claws like small knives sprang forth from each of his eight legs. There was no way I could deflect them all.

I crouched and tucked into a forward roll. I managed to evade Baaz's attack, but at the cost of inter-rupting my spell.

As I stood, I came face to face with an oncoming ball of fiery light.

"Aaaah!" My body reflexively hit the deck. The ball of light whooshed by, scattering crimson flames across the grove of trees behind us.

Vrumugun had cast a fireball!

Rahanim targeted Lantz and descended for him as quickly as he could without ramming into a tree.

Gourry leapt sideways and squatted, drawing a slender needle from his pocket and pricking the hilt of his sword to release the metal fitting that held the blade in place.

"Gaa!" Goluas rushed toward him. A normal sword might be able to harm Goluas, but it wasn't going to do substantial damage. Still, as soon as he caught sight of the unfastened blade, he took advantage of the situation to charge an unarmed Gourry.

But rather than evade, Gourry turned himself to face his attacker head-on.

"Light come forth!" he called, and a blade of glittering light shot out from the empty hilt. *That* was a blade capable of destroying a Mazoku utterly. Gourry raised high the legendary Sword of Light!

"Gwaah!" Compared to his name, the demon-troll let out a rather timid whelp as he folded.

One down!

But before we could get too caught up in the celebrating, Gourry leapt left, and a dozen flaming arrows scorched the spot where he'd been standing a moment before. The lesser demons had joined the attack.

Ah, man! Just when we were making progress.

I looked around and caught Lantz leading the flying fish in some kind of bob-and-weave maneuver. He almost looked like he was having fun . . . or as much fun as you can have running for your life from an airborne flounder, I guess.

The spider-guy was coming for me once again. I dodged, somehow ending up beside Eris, who was trying to quietly sneak out of the area while both sides were ignoring her.

If only I had time to teach that girl a lesson.

Baaz's next attack sent me scurrying again. I hated being on the run, but I knew I couldn't take on an eight-limbed creature with my short sword—and win.

The man-spider eased sideways toward Eris, every step or so glancing in her direction.

Does he think I can't tell he's targeting her?

"Well, hello there!" he said, raising one of his feet high in front of her as if to wave.

Eris froze.

Then—

"I told you to *stop*, Baaz!!" Vrumugun screamed so hard his cheeks nearly burst.

Baaz paused for a moment, licking his lips. "C'mon! Just let me have this *one*. She's little—I'll swallow her whole and be back in the fight before you've missed me."

"Your target is getting *away!*" Vrumugun shrieked just a moment too late.

Their discord was too good an opportunity to let slip. Eris had bought me just enough time to complete my spell: "Blast Ash!"

DOOOOOM! With a heavy sound, the spell I'd fired transformed two lesser demons—along with Vrumugun, who'd been standing right beside them—into unthreatening little piles of black ash.

Baaz's face fell as he realized the caliber of opponent he was facing. His many legs began to quiver.

Eris snapped out of her rigor and hurriedly moved aside.

Though we remained at a disadvantage, the odds had shifted considerably in our favor.

"Gwooooah!" Baaz let out a frenzied war cry. I dodged his charge again and again, each time moving closer to Lantz.

I was hoping he could buy me enough time to cast another spell, but Lantz was fully engaged in his own battle.

Evading Rahanim's attacks hadn't been so tough on its own—what with the trees slowing him down—but the lesser demons had joined in the fray, launching sporadic attack spells from their hiding places.

Lousy cowards . . .

Gourry's situation was even worse.

Speaking in a ghastly demon tongue, Vizea was directing his spineless soldiers to trigger attacks from four sides while he fired his own spells toward Gourry. I don't know if there was another warrior in the world who would have been able to evade them all.

"Goluas! Shockwave!" Vizea ordered.

Goluas?! But he . . .

Goluas had apparently escaped the full brunt of Gourry's earlier attack. He nodded at his master, then took in a deep breath, turning toward Lantz, who still had his hands full with Rahanim and the lesser demons.

Lantz doesn't see him.

"Lan—" Before I could get the word out, Baaz leapt into my face. Goluas, right behind Lantz now, opened his mouth wide and . . .

SPLACK! His body scattered in all directions.

"What the—?!" Vizea shouted as one of the lesser demons went up in a flash of light and disappeared— *poof!*

How could . . . ? That had to be an exorcism spell. It would take a high-ranking priest to cast that . . .

Ohhhh. Nice entrance.

"Sorry to keep you waiting," said the man who had suddenly appeared before us. He was young, with silver hair and a body covered with a pure white poncho. His complexion was the color and texture of blue-black stone, but he was not a golem. Long ago, under the guise of granting him power, the Red Priest had transformed this man into a chimera, combining him with a golem and a blow demon. In pain and regret, he had turned against his master and joined forces with *us.*

"You're late, Zelgadiss." I grinned at our old friend from behind the man-spider's back.

"Hmph!" Tired and afraid, Baaz spun around wildly and came right at me.

I laughed as I took a single step to my right. Homoarachnid slipped past my flank, then wobbled and fell to the ground as though I'd littered the forest floor with banana peels.

"Wh-what happened?" Baaz moaned. Save for a few small quivers, he was unable to move his body at all.

Baaz had failed to notice his *other* new opponent, who had cast a clerical Laphas Seed Shield on me just then.

I finished Baaz off with a Mono Volt spell, at the same time a pretty woman of about twenty years of age appeared from within the forest. I figured she was probably the high priest's daughter who was working with Zel.

"Introductions are gonna have to wait for later," I said to her with a smile.

She wore velvet vestments and had long, black hair, and if I were a man, I would have fallen in love with her right then.

***

The battle had turned decisively in our favor, but Vizea, Rahanim, and a lesser demon still remained.

"What now, then?" Zelgadiss addressed our foes. "Though I have no intention of allowing you to escape, I've no interest in finishing off a weakened force either."

"Escape?" Vizea scoffed. "I return those words to you."

"I admire your confidence," Zelgadiss laughed. "But surely you see your situation is bleak, considering your dwindled numbers."

"It is, considering," Vizea smirked.

Oh, no . . .

I jumped in while the demon nodded. "Zel, he's not worried about his numbers."

"Meaning he expects reinforcements?" Zelgadiss laughed again. "You're bluffing. You're the only minions Rezo has left in Sairaag."

"Minions, you say?" came a voice from the woods.

Oh . . . Holy . . . Crap.

All three of us—Gourry, Zelgadiss, and I—froze in our bones. A chill ran down my spine. We knew that voice all too well.

"My apologies for my late arrival, Mr. Vizea."

"You need not expend words upon me," the Mazoku replied, bowing deeply.

Slowly, we turned to face him . . . a lone man clothed in robes red as blood.

The Red Priest . . . *Rezo.*

3: HURRY UP AND WAIT

"Rezo!" The priestess who had appeared with Zelgadiss spat out his name like a curse.

"Now, now, Miss Sylphiel," the Red Priest chided, his right hand beckoning her as his left hand gripped his priest's staff tight. A bell fitted to the tip of the stick made a soft chime.

This Rezo appeared just as the illusion we had seen in the forest, with both eyes firmly shut and his face shrouded by a red hood.

"If you had continued as Sairaag's quiet priestess, you would have spared yourself these difficulties," Rezo taunted.

"Should I have let you drug me into submission like you did my father?! Don't be absurd!" Sylphiel was defiant.

"My, my. So ugly, these deeds you accuse me of." The priest remained cool in the face of her anger.

"No," I muttered under my breath.

"No what?" He turned toward me and smiled.

"No, you are not Rezo," I said, pointing as I spoke. Sure, his aura matched that of the Rezo I remembered, but there was something off.

"Oh really? I'm not?" the Red Priest raised one eyebrow. He was unperturbed. In fact, he was amused.

"You *can't* be the real Rezo!" I insisted.

There. Guess I told him.

"Well, as much fun as I'm having in this thoughtful debate," he said, pointing his staff at me and punctuating the gesture with a soft chime, "it seems there is a more important matter than whether I am who I say I am. Namely, whether or not you can defeat me."

"We can," I replied without hesitation. "We can, and we have. Whoever you are, you're no more powerful than the real Red Priest."

"Is that what you think?" He growled, his tone betraying his fury for the first time. "Try me!"

I had already begun casting my spell, and the man calling himself Rezo just stood and stared.

"Fireball!" I shouted.

I wanted to test him first. If he was an ordinary man unworthy of the name of Rezo, then one shot would be enough to finish him and there was no point in overkill.

He displayed no reaction whatsoever. No fear, no scorn . . . he just stood there. Silently.

Hmm . . .

I wasn't gonna let my guard down, just the same.

The sphere of light I'd blasted sped straight for the Red Priest's pretender.

". . . ⊨ . . ." The pretender muttered something decidedly foreign, then, pointing the tip of his staff forward, drew a circle in midair. The moment the fireball contacted the circle it vanished, leaving nary so much as an ash.

"Surely you can do better than *that?*" he said, sounding extraordinarily satisfied with himself. I stared speechless.

Then I heard the recitation of a spell on the wind.

Zelgadiss!

"Try this," Zel roared. "Goz Vu Rou!"

With that, a black shadow appeared on the ground between them, and began advancing toward the pretender.

117

The phony Red Priest answered, stabbing the shadow with his staff as it crept near him. There was a sound like the sizzle of water on a hot iron, and the shadow disappeared.

"My turn," the fake Rezo declared, as he began reciting a spell that was familiar to me.

That's Mega Brand . . .

No sooner had I thought it, than the priest added, "Mega Brand it is, but I think you'll agree I've improved upon it somewhat."

Mega Brand is a spell that has been known to create an explosion at ground level. Though an unlucky person could die from a direct hit or from the resulting fall, it doesn't usually inflict fatal wounds. It's nothing to laugh at though, just the same.

"Everyone! Gather around!" I ordered. "Zel! I'll take Wind!"

"Right!" Zelgadiss agreed. Anticipating my plan, he'd already begun casting his spell.

Eris, who'd been attempting to escape, found herself being dragged to safety, by the scruff of her neck by Gourry.

For her part, Sylphiel was chanting a clerical defense.

The ground at our feet began to rumble.

I completed my spell first, and Wind enveloped all of us. Next, Sylphiel's defensive energy surrounded the wind barrier. Finally, Zelgadiss completed his spell, strengthening the wind barrier several times over.

But we weren't in the clear yet. A Mega Brand was coming right at our feet; regardless of its strength, no defensive barrier was going to be adequate against an explosion directly under it. So, I started casting a levitation spell to lift us off the ground and complete our defense. The idea was for the bunch of us to float slowly above the ground in a big soap bubble made out of wind.

But the phony Rezo finished his spell first.

Damn! Just a little longer and . . .

I kept thinking it was completely my fault. I should have left the wind barrier to Zelgadiss and cast Levitation first.

I braced for the attack, but he wasn't attacking. It was as though he was waiting for us to get ready.

I completed my spell. Awkward and unsteady, the wind barrier began to float into the sky. As it slowly rose, I saw our enemy raise his staff high and bring it down hard.

The earth rumbled.

The ground was ripped asunder, blown straight up. Leaves scattered as tree trunks and bushes were sent flying, roots and all. Stones, soil, and countless tiny bits of debris crashed hard into our bubble, and we felt it.

At least Vizea and Rahanim were nowhere to be seen. We figured they must have run off when the fake Rezo physically came onto the scene.

Our bubble barrier began to shake violently from the full-force impact of pieces of an old cart.

"Ouch!" Lantz yelped out suddenly.

"What was that?!" Gourry asked, and then calmed himself. "It was a pebble . . . just a pebble. It's okay."

Wait a minute . . .

Obviously, the color of Zelgadiss' face couldn't tell me anything, but the color of Sylphiel's face had definitely changed.

. . . The barrier's broken.

It had taken one hell of a lot of power to destroy *that* defense. Whoever this guy was, he wasn't messing around. A "somewhat improved Mega Brand" was a considerable understatement. That spell might have brought down a wyvern.

The earth continued to rumble as black smoke rose from it steadily. A large crater of red earth had been carved out of the surface of the forest, a solitary red silhouette standing at its center. His demeanor calm, the man who claimed to be the Red Priest silently raised his head.

"It would seem wise to beat a temporary retreat," Sylphiel suggested.

"Yeah . . . yeah," I quietly agreed. We had three people with us who had no defense against magic. For their sakes—as well as our own—it seemed we had no other choice.

Sure, Gourry was capable of dodging small spells, and he could probably knock off a few more with the Sword of Light, but Lantz and Eris . . . Lantz and Eris were too vulnerable. We'd have to get them to safety and rethink our plan.

"Where, though?" I wondered aloud. "Can anybody think of a place to hide out?"

Sylphiel looked at me and smiled. "I know just the place," she said.

"Let's hope we can get there safely," Zelgadiss interjected, referring to the false Red Priest still on the ground.

It was clear from looking at Zel that the fear and pressure from the battle against the real Rezo still weighed heavily on his heart. And after witnessing the titanic display of magical power we'd just seen, the idea that our opponent might actually be the genuine article must have crossed his mind. I know it did mine.

"At any rate, we'll have to try," I said, steering the damaged bubble as well as I could.

But . . . why wasn't the Red Priest pursuing us? He was only watching, allowing our escape. I didn't understand it then, but I knew it was pointless to ponder. For whatever reason, he was giving us this opportunity, and we had no choice but to take it. Summoning every bit of mental strength I could manage, I somehow increased our speed, and for a brief moment, the wind blew up the hood that kept the Red Priest's features shrouded. In that moment, I thought I saw something red shining against the backdrop of his white skull.

Hmm . . .

***

By the time I felt safe enough to take a deep breath, we were in something like a small hall. The air had that same damp chill you'd find in a cave. Actually, it *was* a cave of sorts. Thanks to the phosphorescent moss growing all over the walls and ceiling and the countless faerie souls fluttering about, the hall was bright as day.

Okay, well, not like a super sunshiny day or anything. But you know, it was bright. For a cave.

Is everyone here familiar with faerie souls? That's what we call those little balls of light that drift around in caves like

this. They're about the size of your fingertip and they look similar to fireflies.

When I was little, my big sister would take me to see them when autumn came around, and I was sad to see the fireflies go away. Unlike lightning bugs, though, if you catch a faerie soul, no matter how slowly and carefully you open your hand, you'll find it empty.

I have no idea if they really are *souls,* as the name implies. No one knows. I think the Sorcerers' Guild is looking into it, but really, who cares? They're harmless and they look nice, so there you go. That particular cave had more than I'd ever seen. It must have been some kind of nest for them.

Anyway, we'd escaped—or we'd been allowed to escape—and, following Sylphiel's directions, we'd walked nearly to death, meandering down tunnels leading right, left, and ever deeper until we finally came to this place. When we finally felt safe—or safe-ish—it was time to talk.

"So you've been following me again." Zelgadiss started in on Eris, the self-styled bounty hunter.

"Oh, shut up. I'm not here because I want to be. He dragged me!" she said, pointing to Gourry. "I was trying to go the other way!"

She'd been trying to escape while the Red Priest was casting his spell.

"Yeah, well," Gourry stammered defensively. "I figured it was too late to make a run for it at that point."

He was trying to save your butt, toots.

"I agree," Sylphiel said. "You couldn't have escaped on foot at that point."

Eris' face took on a pouty look that made me want to slap her, then she sighed and turned the other way.

Gourry looked at Sylphiel, who responded with a deep bow. "Master Gourry," she said, "it is good to see you after such a long time. Please forgive me for not saying so sooner."

"Uh, sure. That's okay," Gourry replied rather meekly, and scratched his face.

"You two know each other?" I asked.

"Sorta," Gourry said simply.

Sorta?

"Rather dreadful things seem to have happened since we saw you last. Have you heard about Father?" Sylphiel continued.

"No I haven't." Gourry looked pained.

"Father, you say?" I interjected.

"I heard you say he was drugged, I think," Gourry went on, completely ignoring me.

Um . . . hello? Can I get a little attention over here?

"Yes, drugged," Sylphiel said (also ignoring me, I might add). "Probably with an extract of vydess root."

"Hey Gourry," I said, trying the direct approach.

"Why would anyone do such a thing?" he continued.

Grrr . . .

I shouldn't have cared. I mean, really, I shouldn't have. But I did.

"Dammit, you two!" Lantz shouted.

Lantz. Not me: Lantz.

"Don't cut us out like that!" he went on.

Everyone else immediately fell silent.

"You two are going on and on and leaving the rest of us totally in the dark! As long as our lives are on the line, don't you think you should explain who's who and what's what—starting with *her*—before the two of you start catching up on old times?!"

"Yeah, what he said!" I chimed in—doing my part, ya know—for the team.

Gourry apologized and explained that he had come to know Sylphiel and her father, the city's high priest, on a previous visit to Sairaag. Apparently there'd been some sort of complicated incident. Neither he nor Sylphiel would give us any details; they only said it had nothing whatsoever to do with the current issue.

No sweat. I'll squeeze the story out of Gourry later.

Anyway, concerning the current matter . . .

The supposed Rezo the Red Priest had arrived in Sairaag a month before with the sorcerer Vrumugun in tow, and everything had gone downhill from there.

Not knowing Rezo's true face, only the stories of the Wandering Sage, the high priest, that is, Sylphiel's father, had welcomed the visitor into his home with open arms.

Impersonating a famous person whose appearance is not well-known has *always* been a good way to swing a free meal.

Apparently, the high priest bought it completely.

I mean, it's great to be generous and all, but if you can't tell something's hinky when an arch-villain shows up at your door, you're pretty much getting what you deserve.

Of course, I wasn't going to say that in front of Sylphiel. What am I, cruel?

And anyway, in fairness, the arch-villain in question was proving to be a pretty good actor.

So, not long after he'd arrived in the city and convinced everyone that he was a living saint, he spoke to the high priest about putting out a bounty on us. The high priest and Sylphiel were completely shocked. Two of the people on the poster were strangers, but the third, Gourry Gabriev, was considered nothing less than the savior of the city.

Hey, way to go, Gourry!

The Rezo character fed them some line about how he was under the control of an evil sorceress—meaning me!

Sylphiel interrupted the story there. "He also said that the sorceress, who looked like a young girl, was in fact an old woman, ninety years of age. Is that part true?" she asked, blinking her long eyelashes in my direction.

"NO! Like hell! I'm sixteen! SIXTEEN!!" I squawked.

"I thought you said you were fifteen?" Gourry asked, suspiciously.

"We passed my birthday! Jeez, I *am* getting older, you know! I'm human."

"I wonder," he mumbled.

Damn that Rezo guy, acting all nice and humble while spreading horrible lies about innocent young girls. *I'll get you for this, Red Priest! I'll get you!*

"I'm so sorry! It does seem rather unlikely, doesn't it?" Sylphiel followed up, noticing my keen displeasure. "It's just that I had heard that you were called the Bandit Slayer and the Black Witch, and that you'd destroyed castles and slain kings. I thought that one so accomplished must be older than your years."

You need to know how to quit when you're ahead, sister.

Anyway, this Rezo guy had included the "wanted alive" condition with the bounty on account of Sylphiel and her pop being concerned about Gourry.

The whole thing had been a massive headache for Zelgadiss right from the start. It had been his ill fortune to be near Sairaag when the spectacular bounty was announced, which meant bounty hunters were popping out from behind every corner. And Eris was one of them.

She and Zelgadiss encountered each other again and again—mainly because he had shown restraint and not used the full force that would have gotten rid of her permanently.

Having heard that the bounty had been placed on him by someone in Sairaag who called himself "Rezo," he headed for the source, and Eris stubbornly pursued.

It was a short time after that that Gourry and I found out about the bounties on our own heads. And around that same time, something strange happened in Sairaag: the high priest fell ill. He began to lose weight rapidly and took to mumbling incoherently to himself. He would visit Rezo's room from time to time, his demeanor mysteriously brightening when he emerged, but he only sank deeper into sickness later. Sylphiel began to suspect that Rezo had been drugging her father, so she asked the other priests to investigate, but they all sided with the newcomer. His charisma had forged more than half the city's occupants into fanatical followers.

Or he might have used magic. Who knows?

Regardless, the Red Priest began to assemble an unorthodox force, including a fish-man and even a Mazoku. No one in town raised an objection or demonstrated concern.

Then, just as Sylphiel was feeling completely isolated and utterly helpless, Zelgadiss appeared.

The two plotted to assassinate the Rezo figure, but the Mazoku Vizea thwarted their plans, so they fled Sairaag City together. After delivering the body blow that halted Eris' persistent pursuit, they headed deeper into the forest, where they heard what sounded like a series of attack spell explosions, and they decided to investigate. And that's how we all met up.

"I knew you'd find out about the bounty and come this way eventually," Zelgadiss said.

"Hey, *I'm* the real victim here!" Eris interrupted our lovefest. "I mean, why'd I have to get dragged here with you people?! It's not like I thought the Red Priest was just gonna pay me my reward and send me on my way, but I didn't have any gripe with him either. I mean, I shouldn't be here! I'm leaving. Which way is out?"

Zelgadiss gave her a frosty stare. "Unfortunately, we cannot allow you to leave."

"Wh-why not?" Eris asked, intimidated.

"Because you'd go and tell them where we are," he sighed.

"No, no I wouldn't," she whined.

"Wouldn't you? Rezo's people must be scouring the entire area by now," Zelgadiss explained. "You'd be found, captured, interrogated, and—if you refused to talk—tortured. You could never endure it."

Eris was at a loss for words. She made some small noises inside her mouth and mumbled under her breath before reluctantly sitting back down.

"Where are we, anyway?" I wondered. "I couldn't hang on to any sense of direction back there."

Sylphiel smiled mischievously. "We are in the heart of Sairaag, literally and figuratively. We're inside Flagohn, the Holy Tree."

"We're inside the tree?" I parroted.

"Yes. The Swordsman of Light—Master Gourry's ancestor of many generations ago—fought a battle to the death against the great Demon Beast in this city. Though the beast perished, legend has it that an infinite miasma was released from its dying body.

"The swordsman, riding on a dragon, planted a seedling in the body of the beast to absorb and purify the miasma as it grew. It has now grown to this great height and become the Holy tree, the symbol of our city."

I already knew the story, but it was the first that Lantz and Eris had ever heard of it.

"Oh, so that's what happened," Gourry said, sounding impressed.

I blinked. *You can't be serious.*

"Gourry, how could you *possibly* not know this story? It's about your own ancestor!" I bopped him on the head for emphasis.

"I dunno. I think maybe my father told me the story when I was a little kid," he said. "But I wasn't listening."

Some things never change.

"Anyway," Sylphiel said, pulling herself together and continuing her tale. "The tree's roots grew deep underneath Sairaag and formed many caves like this one. Every cave we traveled through to get here was created by Flagohn's roots."

"So won't Rezo's people in the city know about this place?" I reasoned.

"I think we'll be all right." She giggled. "This tree is considered quite sacred by the townspeople. Though I believe they know about these caves, they would never enter them under ordinary circumstances. And of course there are no maps, so even if they came into the caves to search for us, they would never be able to find us.

"I know my way around because I spent my entire childhood exploring the inside of this tree."

Sylphiel must've been a handful when she was a kid.

"I don't understand how it could be so big," I said, marveling at the size of the hall as I spoke. "Trees that have lived for thousands of years don't have this kind of space inside them. And, according to the legend of the Swordsman of Light, this tree hasn't been here that long."

"Miss Lina, did you look out over the city from the bubble as we made our escape?" she asked.

"Sure, I saw it." I'd glanced at Sairaag on the way in. The city itself radiated out around an enormous central forest with a large plaza surrounding it, with curved rows of houses around that. It was a city shaped like a doughnut, with a forest for a hole.

Wait, no—she couldn't mean . . .

"At the center of the city is our Holy Tree. Many people mistake it for a forest the first time they see it."

"Seriously?!" Lantz and I both yelled out at once.

"H-how old is this thing?" I couldn't believe it.

"This tree takes in evil and malice as nourishment for growth. The greater the miasma, the greater the nourishment, and the faster and larger it grows," she explained.

"Wait, shouldn't the evil spirit of the Demon Beast *hurt* the tree and make it wither?" Lantz asked.

I answered him myself. "It won't wither. Not as long as people live here, it won't."

Sylphiel nodded sadly as Lantz tried desperately to parse my meaning.

"For as long as humanity exists, we will give birth to conflict, sorrow, and enmity. It's a burden that all living things are fated to bear," Sylphiel explained. "For instance, the fish that I ate for supper yesterday must have felt fear and despair at the moment it was pulled from the water. Those negative emotions, in turn, provide nourishment for the tree.

"There is one thing that is weighing on my mind, however," she said, lowering her voice. "May I share it with you, please?" At her request, we listened . . .

And we heard it. Faintly. It was a heavy creaking sound.

"That is the sound of this tree growing." She looked to me, Gourry, and finally Zelgadiss. "Ever since Rezo arrived, it's been growing faster. Please, tell me—*what is he?*"

No one spoke.

There was no way I was going to tell her the truth. It wasn't a matter of whether I trusted her or not. I just didn't want to send her into a panic. For one thing, the matter of whether that Rezo was the real one or not wasn't settled.

"That cannot possibly be the malice and hatred of a mere human being," she said. "A person's mind isn't capable of containing the level of bile that would be required to make the tree grow at this rate."

"To be completely honest, we're not sure what he is either," Gourry answered in a lighthearted tone.

Well, he's not exactly lying.

We didn't know if he was real or an impostor. And if he was an impostor, who was he? And what did he want?

"Whatever he is," Gourry said calmly, "in the end, we have no option but to fight . . . and win."

"Well, certainly," Sylphiel said. The look on her face told me she knew we were leaving out parts of the story. But she respected us enough to let it go.

I changed the subject. "Anyway, since we have no choice but to fight, we have a few important things to take care of first. Namely, what we're going to *eat* and where we're going to *get it*."

Gourry and Zelgadiss looked pained as I spoke.

"That's not where I thought she was going with that," Lantz said.

"Me, either." Eris chimed in, sounding dour.

"I do not think we need to be concerned," Sylphiel explained. "There are mushrooms that grow a little farther down. I'm certain that they're edible."

"Yay, mushrooms!" I squealed.

"So I guess we should all go pick mushrooms?" Lantz sounded perplexed.

"Shouldn't we think of a plan first?" Zelgadiss ventured, raining on my mushroom parade.

"Yeah," Gourry agreed. "We should settle on a few things before we go any further."

"I concur," Sylphiel concurred. "The mushrooms will still be there once we've made our decisions."

"Precisely," Zelgadiss said, sounding pleased. "We haven't earned the luxury of feeding our bellies just yet."

"Well, I'm not exactly dying to go pick mushrooms," Eris offered. She must have been feeling left out, the witch.

I wilted under the brunt of sudden opposition. "All right, all right! Jeez! You don't need to go ganging up on me like that. You want to plan our next move? Let's plan our next move, then."

My stomach rumbled and I was irritated. "Where do we stand? Well, we don't know our enemy's true nature. Everyone in the city is his ally, and the chances of us being spotted are dangerously high. Okay, people, that's where we stand. Now what actions can we take under these circumstances? Besides waiting for our opponent to make the next move, I mean?"

"Huh? Oh. Well . . ." Zelgadiss was reaching.

"Sylphiel?" I looked at her highness.

"Um . . . well . . ."

"So you agree with Zel? Great . . ." I looked to Lantz and Eris, who shook their heads before I could call on them.

Jeez . . .

There was only Gourry left.

"Gourry probably hasn't been thinking at all." I sighed.

"I've got an opinion," he said, his tone brimming with confidence.

Ohhh!

Everyone looked at him cautiously.

"What kind of opinion?" I asked.

Gourry lifted a finger in response to my question. "It is my opinion that we should all go pick mushrooms."

My foot slammed into his face.

***

"Why does stuff like this always have to happen to *me?*" Eris whined.

"Why can't I get a *nice* welcome once in a while? I've really stuck my foot in it this time," Lantz grumbled to no one in particular.

"Maybe I'm just aiming too high, but if I didn't work so hard, I wouldn't get into these messes," Eris mumbled to herself.

"I mean, a Mazoku. A *Mazoku!*" Lantz went on. "Do we really have enough firepower to take on a guy who can control a dozen lesser demons without breaking a sweat?"

"This sucks!" Eris summed it up.

"Silence!" I yelled at last, rising to my feet. "Lantz! Eris! You're pathetic!"

"But—"

"Hey—"

They both looked at me like I'd betrayed them.

Jeez!

Once things had calmed down, Sylphiel had shown us all to a spot where we could pick mushrooms. This cave was a little larger and the lighting a little weaker than the last one, which gave the place a gloomy feel.

"It *is* rather pitiful, certainly," Zelgadiss grumbled, which was rare for him.

"Well, I suppose it is unusual for swordsmen and priestesses and sorceresses to be picking mushrooms together," Sylphiel added in a melancholic tone.

"Stop grumbling, all of you! Oh, Zelgadiss," I said while continuing to pick. "I forgot to ask about Vrumugun."

"What's wrong, Eris?" Lantz had noticed a sour look on Eris' face.

"Nothing. Just some weird insect," she said, batting at the air like a kitten.

"Lantz, Eris: can you be quiet for a minute? I'm talking about something important."

They both shrugged their shoulders and went back to picking mushrooms.

I returned my attention to Zelgadiss.

"There was a sorcerer with Rezo called Vrumugun, right? Do you know anything about him at all?" I asked. He should at least have heard of the sorcerer before. After all, he himself had formerly served the real Rezo.

"Ah, *him*," he said with a tedious tone.

"You knew him?"

"I knew *of* him. So, how many times have *you* killed him?" Zelgadiss inquired.

"You mean—?!"

"He has no distinguishing features whatsoever. Other than the name he claims for himself and the ruby implanted in his forehead, I know nothing of him. Every time I am certain I've destroyed him utterly, he reappears unexpectedly. This happens again and again," Zelgadiss said with resignation in his voice.

"You've killed him multiple times, too?"

"Five . . . no, six times maybe?" Zelgadiss looked up and counted from memory. "Once, I not only confirmed his death, but I also burned his remains to ash with a fireball and tossed the ashes into a river."

"I hadn't quite gotten to that point yet," I said, impressed.

"I thought he might be undead," Zelgadiss explained.

So that was it.

The term *undead* covered not only low-ranking zombies but also vampire-class types who refused to die no matter how many times you killed them. Zelgadiss was trying to make sure that the guy couldn't revive himself even if he was undead.

Of course, some undead are spirited enough that even burning their corpses and performing a ceremony over their ashes isn't enough to stop them from reviving. To truly destroy *those* requires a priest's Exorcism spell, or—just like with Mazoku—you can strike them at their source from the astral plane.

"But he came back no matter what you did?"

"Yes," Zelgadiss sighed. "Honestly, I only ever heard the old Rezo use the name Vrumugun once."

"Oh?"

"Yes. It was at a time when I was certain he was going to praise me. Instead, he warned me, 'Do not show conceit. There are two sorcerers under my command whose sorcery is greater than yours.'"

"And Vrumugun was one of them?" I asked.

"Yes, but he never said anything more about it. Honestly, it was at that point that I began to realize that I hoped to destroy him one day."

"And the other sorcerer?"

"He never mentioned the name."

"Hmm, I see." There were all sorts of hypotheses fluttering around inside my head. "So, before this incident, you'd never met Vrumugun in person?"

"I had not."

"So, if the Vrumugun that we've been defeating isn't the real one, you wouldn't know?" I was finally beginning to understand the sorcerer's true nature.

"What do you mean?" Zelgadiss looked puzzled.

"Think about it," I said. "What's he got for distinguishing features? Medium build, a black mantle, and a deep hood you could buy at a used clothing store in any small town, right? Plus the ruby in his forehead.

"Except for the ruby, none of those characteristics is very distinguishing. In fact, it raises the question as to whether they're indistinct *on purpose.*"

I'm a genius. I really am.

"Yes, I see," Zelgadiss said, finally grasping my genius. "The ruby."

"Yep, the ruby."

"What about the ruby?" Lantz wanted to know. "I don't get it."

Oh, oops. I forgot anyone else was listening.

"Ah," I said, coughing before continuing—for emphasis, you know, "I'm suggesting that the Vrumuguns we've been defeating have all been fakes, and the real one's controlling them through the rubies implanted in their foreheads."

"He could do that?" Lantz looked horrified.

"He could," I replied matter-of-factly.

It's a form of mind control. A person's mind can be controlled through a Black Magic curse or by attaching an object to his body and performing a lengthy ritual.

"The victim would usually revert to normal if the spell caster quit concentrating, but that wouldn't happen if, say, one had a magically enchanted ruby planted in one's forehead.

"When Rezo said that Vrumugun's sorcery was greater, he didn't necessarily mean he could use more powerful attack spells.

"From the first moment I laid eyes on Vrumugun I figured him for third-rate. In all likelihood, though, the real Vrumugun's power is much greater than the abilities of those he controls with his rubies. So, the real one's been sending fake Vrumuguns with the same undistinguishable features to harass us and make us think they're all the same person. Get it?"

"So, who's the real Vrumugun?" Eris asked.

"We can't be sure at this stage, but I think the real Vrumugun might have a ruby implanted in his own body to control the fakes, and I'm pretty sure that I saw something red embedded in the forehead of the guy calling himself Rezo.

"So, let's think about this: We've got a man named Rezo who can't be the real Rezo because the real Rezo has to be dead; and we have a sorcerer whose face no one knows who calls himself Vrumugun. What does that suggest?" I put the question to the group.

"You mean the fake Rezo's the real Vrumugun?" said Gourry, of all people.

You can think, you dumb lug! I'm so proud!

"Aren't you forgetting something, though?" Lantz said, gnawing on a mushroom baked over a fire spell of mine. "How to beat them, I mean."

The cave was filled with a flickering light, and the scent of baked mushrooms drowned out all other smells.

Damn you, Lantz. You've got a point.

Having finally figured out who Vrumugun was, all we were doing was picking mushrooms. Considered like that, it did seem silly.

"We should actually back up even further," Zelgadiss said, glancing at Lantz and Eris, "to the matter of how much combat capability these two possess."

"Hey, now just a—" Lantz shot Zel an angry look. "You're not suggesting *she and I* take those guys on?!"

"If you are, you can forget it," Eris said, shaking her head in a fluster.

"That is not what I am suggesting," Zelgadiss said simply. "Because despite your boasts, you haven't the means to oppose an enemy whose main force is comprised of Mazoku. Unless, of course, you've been withholding a secret weapon?"

Lantz fell silent.

Damn, Zel. That was pretty harsh.

He was right, though. Zelgadiss, Sylphiel, and I had magic, and Gourry could defeat Mazoku with the Sword of Light. But Lantz . . . Lantz hadn't been able to contribute anything to the previous battle because he didn't have a weapon that was effective against Mazoku.

"Don't worry!" I said, trying to bolster his confidence. "You can manage anything if you've got guts!"

"Yeah, right." Lantz sounded downright dejected.

"Seriously!" I said, but the look on his face remained dour. "Lantz, seriously—look at me: I'm not kidding." I guess my lighthearted tone had made him think I was mocking him.

"Seriously?" he repeated.

"*Seriously*," I said seriously. "Look, Mazoku exist primarily on the astral plane. That's why attacking them physically doesn't do any damage.

"See, they're basically unbeatable in a straight-up fight. The only way to defeat a Mazoku is to destroy its spirit.

"So for example, if you were to concentrate on your intention to destroy a Mazoku at the moment you hit it with a sword, if that sword had the power of will in it, you'd do some damage—even up against a Mazoku of greater mental power.

"That's why silver weapons are so effective against ghosts and stuff—because silver conducts will much better than steel.

"And Gourry's Sword of Light! That's how it works. It takes human willpower and amplifies it to create its blade."

"Really?" Gourry said, looking at the sword on his hip as if seeing it for the first time.

I wonder if he was dropped on his head as a child . . . that might explain it.

"So, anything that would amplify a person's mental power would work, then?" Lantz asked, wanting to make sure he was following my logic.

I brought both my hands together in a clap, cutting off Sylphiel as she tried to get a word in. "That's the short version, yeah."

"I agree," Sylphiel added.

"Seriously?!" Lantz brightened.

Seriously, dude.

"Long ago, a sword was discovered within Flagohn," Sylphiel went on. "It is said that the sword was born of the tree itself. It resonates with the same energy as the Holy Tree and is capable of purifying and amplifying the bearer's will. It was presented to the city in the temple, but . . ."

"But what?!" *Come on! You can't just leave a girl hanging!*

"But when I was a child, I stole it and hid it in this cave as a prank," she continued.

Wow, you really were a little pistol, weren't you?

"Didn't the city freak out?" I asked eagerly.

"The city most certainly did 'freak out,' " she said awkwardly. "I was so frightened and overwhelmed by their reaction that I was afraid to return the sword and risk discovery. However, it now seems that my childhood prank will serve a purpose."

For someone who spoke so formally, Sylphiel was turning out to be quite a character.

"All right, what are we waiting for? Let's all go and get it!" I said, rallying the troops.

"No," Sylphiel said, quickly putting the kibosh on that idea. "I do not think that would be best."

Just when I was starting to like this girl.

"There are many narrow passages that like the ones here are poorly lit and difficult to maneuver through. If we were to all go, and something unfortunate were to

happen, we would trample one another in the course of battle or escape," she explained. "I must go, of course, with one other, while the rest of you stay behind. Master Gourry, would you accompany me?"

"Me?" Gourry asked, and he glanced over at me for some reason.

She liiiikes you, she liiiikes you! Heh heh heh. No accounting for taste, I guess.

"We should get going," Sylphiel said, and she rose to her feet. "It would be best to do this soon."

Gourry, still looking a bit unenthused, got up and put a hand on my shoulder. "Don't do anything stupid while I'm gone," he said.

"Who me? I'll be fine. Trust me." I laughed. It was sweet of him to be concerned.

"You're not exactly trustworthy," he continued.

Scratch that *sweet* bit, would you?

"All right, well—the sooner we go, the sooner we get back," he said, offering me a clumsy wink as he went off with Sylphiel.

The four of us watched them leave, and with the remaining mushrooms already consumed, we suddenly found ourselves with nothing to do.

"So . . . what now?" Eris asked, sitting cross-legged.

"Er, yeah . . . what now?" Lantz said, looking like he was deep in thought while he actually stole glances at her legs.

"Nothing we can do now but wait," Zelgadiss explained matter-of-factly. "If we went off and tried to do something on our own and something went wrong, we wouldn't be able to recover."

"Couldn't we think up some kind of plan?" Lantz asked, still ogling Eris' gams.

"Remember what Lina said earlier," Zel sighed. "All we can do right now is conserve our strength and wait for the enemy to make a move. Despite Sylphiel's concerns for Gourry, my bet is that Rezo put the 'wanted alive' condition on the bounty so that he could defeat us himself. So, he'll definitely come in person, probably with a small group of minions."

"Well, I'm bored," I announced after all of about thirty seconds. "There's gotta be something we can actually *do*, right?"

"Like?" Lantz was bored too, I could tell.

"We could pick more mushrooms."

"What the hell were you thinking, giving her an opening like that?" Eris kicked Lantz.

"Picking mushrooms gets really old," Lantz agreed, clutching his shin.

I made them pick mushrooms anyway. It's good to be the queen.

"Look, this ensures that we'll have enough food for cooking," I explained, as I examined a particularly hearty fungus. "If you really hate it that much, you should've said *no* from the start and stayed behind like Zelgadiss!"

"But—!" Eris objected, knowing I wouldn't really have let her sit out.

"I figured waiting would have been even worse," reasoned Lantz.

"This sucks," Eris spat.

"Well, put your back into it." Lantz was getting annoyed with her, too.

"Don't tell me how to pick mushrooms!" she shrieked.

And you thought Gourry and *I* were bad.

"All right, you two, enough! What's with the title fight? If you keep this up, I'll eat all the mushrooms and I won't leave any for you!" I threatened and muttered as I kept picking.

What? A growing girl requires sustenance, and I couldn't work with all that kvetching.

"You're acting like little kids! Well, I'm still young too, you know." Just then I sensed a presence behind me, and I turned.

"Lantz!"

Lantz was still standing, but he leaned on the nearest wall for support. He didn't have any obvious wounds, but his left hand was rubbing his forehead, and he had a pained expression on his face.

"What happened?!" A chill ran down my spine. I couldn't put it into words, but I knew something was very wrong. I dropped my mantle, letting the mushrooms fall to the ground.

"It's them," he muttered.

"Who? Where?!" I moved forward. Another chill. I pulled back a step without thinking, and something hot hit my gut. I'd been attacked! I leaned against the wall and checked my wound. I'd been stabbed a little to the left of my navel. I couldn't speak.

Lantz smiled as he held out a bloody knife for me to see, a red ruby glittering in his forehead.

"*Here*," he said, his voice filled with enmity.

Eris had the same smile on her face and a ruby of her own. How long had she been hiding it under her bandanna? She, too, held a knife.

"It is I, Vrumugun," Lantz growled through his grin.

I could bear the burning sensation, but the bleeding wouldn't stop . . .

"Huu!" I sidestepped Lantz's next attack, but I was teetering on my feet. My wound was serious.

This is bad.

I had to take care of it quickly, but I couldn't just blow them away—they didn't know what they were doing!

Wobbly, I tried to move in closer and began quietly chanting a sleeping spell inside my mouth.

"Oh no you don't!" Lantz lunged at me again. I managed to dodge him, but at the price of pausing my spell.

Ugh . . .

I felt something hot in the back of my throat.

Definitely not good.

"It seems this is as far as you go," Eris said with a wry smile. "You can't chant spells while you're coughing up blood."

Shut up, you little brat! My soul shouted. If I lost hope, then it really would be *the end* for me. My left hand drew my short sword from its sheath.

I closed the distance between me and Lantz, swinging wildly.

"Ugh!" I lost my grip as a sharp pain ran through my arms, and my sword slipped from my fingers. The only option

I had left was to run. I grazed by Lantz, heading deeper into the cave, a hard clanging sound ringing behind me.

"You greet death poorly, Lina Inverse," Lantz called out from behind. "You should accept Vrumugun's vengeance peacefully."

Eris, who'd hit my sword arm with a stone, closed in on me, her knife at the ready.

I teetered, and something snagged my foot. Losing my balance I fell ass-over-teakettle backward.

This is it . . .

I lost consciousness.

***

When I came to, I saw a bright light . . . and shadows. I heard them clamoring to each other.

"Oh be quiet," I mumbled and moaned.

One of the shadows said something. What was it? Oh yes, it was telling me not to talk.

I couldn't focus. I opened and closed my eyes, slowly and repeatedly. Gradually, I was able to make out the contours of the shadow with the white light behind it.

Sylphiel?

She was chanting something. It was Resurrection.

I should point out that the spell doesn't actually bring people back to life as the name suggests. For humans, death is final. Resurrection, however, is several steps above the Recovery spell, which is widely known not only to priests, but also to traveling sorcerers, a few warriors, bards, and merchants, even.

A polite request and a small donation is usually enough to get a priest to teach you the spell. Actually, I know it, too.

Anyway, Recovery temporarily increases the speed of a wounded person's natural healing process, but it still comes down to the body's endurance versus the severity of the injury.

Resurrection, on the other hand, acts as a medium for sending energy and power gathered from the surrounding area into the wounded body. Consequently, even a person whose endurance has been completely exhausted can be healed. A high-level priest can use the spell even to regenerate lost limbs.

If she had to use Resurrection, I was in pretty dire straits.

"Lina? You okay? Does it hurt?" Gourry, my self-styled guardian, sounded desperate.

I coughed and nodded. Zelgadiss was watching from behind Gourry.

Beyond them were Lantz and Eris. There was no sign of a ruby on either of them. Lantz looked like he might cry while Eris watched with a sad face.

I didn't know how, but I'd been saved.

"A little while after you left, I heard the sound of a sword falling," Zelgadiss said in a quiet voice. "At first I thought I'd imagined it, but I had a bad feeling about it, so I went to investigate. I found you on the ground and rubies in both their foreheads. Only after I had subdued them and tied them up so they couldn't move did I become aware of your grave wound. I would have been hard-pressed alone, but fortunately, Gourry and Sylphiel returned sooner than expected."

The sound of my dropped sword had echoed inside the cave and alerted Zel.

But, if that was the case, then that meant . . .

"When we tried to talk to Lantz and Eris, they fell into a deep sleep," Zel went on. "Sylphiel broke the spell and removed the rubies from their foreheads. They remembered nothing."

"I was worried," Gourry whispered.

"Mmm . . ." I smiled softly.

"Lina, I am so very sorry!" Lantz wailed from the rear, busting up my tender moment. I waved it off with my hand. It wasn't his fault. Vrumugun was responsible.

Everyone except Sylphiel was silent as her chant reverberated within the cave. I was looking at nothing in particular when my gaze fell upon the sword in Gourry's hands.

"Is that . . . it?" I somehow managed to ask.

"You can speak," Sylphiel remarked with a small sigh, pausing in her chant for a moment. "I am glad of it. But I beg you not to speak more than you must, for now.

"That sword . . . yes, it is the sword born of Flagohn. We refer to it as the Blessed Blade."

"Explain later," Zelgadiss said in his usual flat tone. "Concentrate on healing her right now. Vrumugun knows where we are. We need to get out of here as soon as she can move."

"What would be the point?" a voice asked from afar. It came to us as an echo through the tunnel. It was Rezo!

"You hear me, do you not? I can hear you, you know. I will be creating my own path to you soon. You have been warned."

Then silence.

"Get down!" Zelgadiss yelled out. Everyone hit the dirt at once, doing what we could to take cover.

A light far brighter than the phosphorescent moss made its way into the dome-shaped room where we were.

I knew it.

That was when I knew it for sure.

***

When we finally lifted our heads there was a passage right beside us that was large enough for a tall adult. Really tall. Like, a cyclops or something.

Gourry went over to investigate.

"Lantz," he called back, tossing him the Blessed Blade.

"Yeah?" Lantz said, hoisting the weapon.

"I'm going in. Look after Lina."

Lantz looked up at his face, then nodded firmly. "Count on it."

"Shall we?" Zelgadiss passed Gourry and headed for the tunnel, his familiar broadsword dangling from one hand. He waved back at us without turning his head.

"Well, I can't let him have *all* the fun," Gourry said by way of good-bye, and he took off walking with Zel.

A couple of trolls rushed out of the tunnel. Gourry felled one with a single blow while Zel destroyed the other with an attack spell.

Then . . . they vanished into the tunnel. We heard sounds of sword fighting and explosions, but they grew ever more distant.

"Miss Sylphiel," Lantz said, "keep working on Lina, please. We'll head out as soon as she can move."

"Please be patient. It's going to take a little longer," Sylphiel responded.

"Okay, well . . ." Eris was the next one to raise her voice. "I'm sorry, but this is my exit cue. I'd just be slowing you guys down anyway."

"Eris!" She was already on her way out when a strong voice stopped her mid-step. The voice was mine.

"No. You'll be in danger if you're caught," I said flatly.

"B-but . . ." Eris whined again.

"No. So help me—"

"Lina's right," Lantz said, interrupting my threat. Eris grumbled again and gave up.

I breathed a sigh of relief and shifted my gaze toward the mouth of the tunnel. "They're probably fine, those two . . . right?"

"You should be more concerned about yourselves, if you ask me."

We all turned toward the voice. A figure dressed in black stood facing us.

Vizea.

"This is the perfect opportunity to deal with you," he said, chuckling.

"N-not gonna . . . let you . . ." I tried to get up, but even though the pain had subsided, I was just too weak.

"No, not yet." Sylphiel held me down.

"Lantz . . . Lantz, I'm sorry. I need a little more time. Just until I recover . . ."

"Don't worry, I gotcha." Lantz slowly rose to his feet, the Blessed Blade hanging from one hand. There was a flash of something new in his eyes.

"I'm not just gonna buy you time, Lina. I owe you and I made a promise to big bro, too. So . . ." He held the sword before him. "I'm taking this thing *down.*"

4: CITY OF GHOSTS: ALL THAT REMAINS IS THE WIND

"If your chances weren't so sad, that might be funny," Vizea sneered in a completely contemptuous tone. He seemed insulted that anyone would even consider the possibility that he could be defeated by a human warrior.

"Lantz!" I shouted. "As soon as you get an opening, strike! Put your will into it! You can do this!"

"Nonsense." Vizea chuckled.

Be quiet, you. Don't laugh; it's not funny.

I knew from experience how hard it was to maintain complete concentration in hand-to-hand combat. All Lantz needed was a tiny opening, a little slip. With his willpower infused into the Blessed Blade, he stood a chance. However . . .

Lantz was not exactly famous for his strong will.

Of course, compared to normal people, even the worst of the best is still one of the best. He at least stood a better chance than your average warrior. I didn't know how powerful the Blessed Blade was, but if it could just raise his power a little above Vizea's defenses . . .

"You will die," Vizea promised.

"Eventually, I'm sure." Lantz managed a hearty laugh.

Good show, big guy.

"When I have finished with you, there will be no remains left to identify," Vizea continued with the trash-talking.

"Bring it!" Lantz challenged. Countless white tendrils sprouted from the right side of Vizea's face.

"Hmph!" Lantz grunted as the Blessed Blade swept them aside in a flash. Lantz pressed closer to the Mazoku.

"Kudos!" Vizea leapt high, grabbing onto the ceiling like a giant bug. "You may be more entertaining than I expected."

"Oh, I don't think you'll be enjoying yourself for long," Lantz shot back.

"Is that so?" Vizea let go of the ceiling and dove straight for Lantz. More white whips shot out from the side of his face.

"Dwah!" Lantz threw himself out of the way. Tentacles from Vizea's flesh plunged deep into the floor, his feet landing there a moment afterward.

"Dammit! That's cheating, you weasel!"

"Not a weasel," Vizea chuckled, "a *Mazoku*." Just as he said that, the ground at Lantz's feet split!

"What the—?!"

The Mazoku's tentacles were creeping up from below. Lantz quickly leapt back, away from them. One managed to pierce his lower leg nonetheless.

"Argh!" he cried, swinging his sword down. Even severed, the tentacle continued to invade his flesh. "You bastard!" he swore, "I'm gonna tear you apart!" This time he swung, and when the Blessed Blade touched the tentacle, the tentacle vanished with a loud crack.

Good. His will is growing with his anger. Unfortunately, Vizea's was growing, too.

"What's the matter? Does it *hurt*?" Vizea mocked. Suddenly, the wall beside Lantz burst, and more tentacles reached forth.

Lantz brought his sword down to slice them.

Watching Vizea's attack pattern was making me sick. I decided I wouldn't be eating pasta anytime soon.

"Huh?!" Lantz stopped. The sword in his hand was being pulled in the Mazoku's direction. A thin tentacle had wrapped itself around the Blessed Blade and was attempting to wrench it away from Lantz.

"This game has gone on long enough," Vizea declared. "First, you will give me that blade." Suddenly, a small, groaning sound echoed through the cave. It seemed to be coming from Flagohn itself.

For a moment, Vizea looked around with a suspicious eye, but he soon returned his focus to Lantz.

"A fine blade, indeed," he said, admiringly. "Most magic swords are broken easily by a single tentacle."

There was no way that sword was going to break. As Sylphiel had explained, it was attuned to Flagohn itself. To break it would be to break the tree. Mazoku though he was, Vizea was no threat to that tree. Quite the opposite, in fact.

"If I cannot break it, then I shall have it," he sneered, and the thin tentacle yanked hard.

Lantz let out a small yelp. He was jerked several paces forward, but had managed to hold onto the blade. He drew closer to Vizea, who pulled him with a single, tiny tentacle.

"Oh . . . nooooo!" Lantz suddenly let go of the blade. The recoil sent the Mazoku flying backward.

"Gah!!" The sword that Vizea had so desired went flying for the Mazoku, point first.

Thwook! The Blessed Blade thrust deep into the Mazoku's midsection.

"Take THAT!" Lantz yelled, and Vizea's scream filled the cavern.

"Err . . . gghhh . . ." Vizea raised his right hand slowly. He'd survived the attack!

"Come on! Oh, come ON!" Lantz was trying to pull the sword from the Mazoku's belly.

Vizea's right hand twitched and continued to move.

"Damn! Damn it all to hell!" Lantz cried out in utter exasperation.

"Daa!" Vizea's body bent backward.

Lantz let go and stepped away. The sword remained in the Mazoku's belly.

"Gu . . . fuu . . . haa . . ." The Mazoku's breathing was labored, but a ghastly smile was forming on his face.

"Well done," he said. "Now I shall return the favor." He took one staggering step toward Lantz.

Lantz crept backward. The Mazoku stretched both of his arms out, thrusting the sword, still planted in his gut, toward Lantz like a dare.

"It seems you have forgotten something," he hissed. "Don't you want to retrieve it?" Vizea pressed closer to him still. "What will you do now, hmm?" Vizea was rapidly closing the distance between them.

Without the Blessed Blade, Lantz stood no chance. Knowing this, the Mazoku continued to taunt him.

Lantz put it all on the line and took his only remaining option, charging right at the advancing Vizea, grabbing hold of the sword still plunged into him, and driving all of his will into the Mazoku. If he was struck by Vizea's attacks before doing so, he'd lose. If Vizea managed to resist his will . . . well, he'd lose in that case, too.

It was an uphill battle either way.

Lantz's back hit the wall. The phosphorescent moss was wiped away from that area, leaving one of Flagohn's giant roots exposed. The impact sent spores dancing into the air.

"Come to me!" Vizea called for him.

"Rest in pieces, monster!" Lantz howled.

At that same moment, the Mazoku's body burst into messy chunks.

"Ooo . . . ?" Vizea lay in parts on the ground, his head unable to comprehend what had just happened to the rest of his body.

Instead of blood, yellow dust the color of cheddar cheese spewed from his wound, filling the air with thick clouds of the stuff. Twitching was the only movement he could manage.

With a buzz like the song of a small swarm of insects, his flesh broke down completely. Only some dust and the Blessed Blade remained.

Lantz had driven his will into Flagohn and used the tree itself to smash the Mazoku into pieces.

He glanced in our direction. "Eris? You okay?" He broke her out of her reverie. "What were you just thinking about?"

That's a dangerous question to ask someone, if I do say so myself.

"Ah . . . eh? U-um . . . I was thinking that I've never seen a Mazoku die like that before," she replied in an awkward tone. Just as I'd expected.

***

"Haa!" Gourry cleaved a brass demon in two with a flash of the Sword of Light. The battle was mostly decided.

The tunnel that Rezo had opened into Flagohn continued all the way to the center of Sairaag. A rather large plaza surrounded the tree, and houses large and small stood in neat rows beyond it. We could see a crowd of onlookers watching from there.

Sure must be nice to be one of those people who just gets to stand around and watch. *On second thought . . . nah.*

"I shall not forgive you," said Rahanim, slowly turning about in the sky, setting his sights on Zelgadiss.

"Zelgadiss! Look out!" Gourry yelled, just as Rahanim's form vanished.

Zelgadiss dodged instinctively. The force of the wind clipped his cheek. "I see," he said, licking his lips, his interest piqued. Red blood flowed from a shallow groove in his rock-hard cheek.

"Be careful! This guy gave us a really hard time!" Gourry warned.

"A hard time, you say? You and Lina had a hard time against a fish-man?" Zelgadiss looked like he might laugh at the notion.

"What? He moves so fast that you can't see him to slice him!" Gourry explained.

"Who needs to *see* him?" Zelgadiss asked. So boasting, he thrust his sword directly toward Rahanim as the fish-man floated in the air. "Come on, fellow. I'll be having fish for dinner."

"So you say!" The fish-man's tail flicked suddenly as his form vanished once more.

Zelgadiss moved at the same time, raising his sword, lowering his body, and putting his weight forward.

Now, why didn't I think of that?

Zelgadiss' body pitched backward as we heard a sickening rip. Rahanim had fallen to the ground farther behind him. He'd been sliced evenly in two.

Certainly the speed the fish-man possessed was impressive; but, on the other hand, he had no maneuverability whatsoever. So, if someone lunged the instant he vanished from sight, he could dodge the attack. But with no maneuverability, he couldn't change course or swerve to miss a blade held in the position of his original trajectory.

It was blatantly obvious when I thought about it.

"See?" said Zelgadiss.

Gourry's eyes narrowed.

"Hello there!" Zelgadiss waved a hand in our direction.

"Hi!" I cheerfully waved back.

Gourry finally noticed us. "Your wound all right now?" he called.

"Yeah. Tip-top!" I answered, adding a short nod.

"How long have you been standing there?" Zelgadiss asked.

"Since you faced off against Rahanim. I can't believe I didn't think of that."

It wasn't long after Lantz finished his duel with the demon that I was completely healed. Lantz's wounds were repaired shortly after; and Sylphiel, Eris, Lantz, and I took off after the other two.

"Vrumugun came out again," Zelgadiss began catching us up on what we'd missed, ". . . and was defeated. That leaves the Mazoku Vizea."

"Oh, Lantz took care of him already," I offered casually.

"*Lantz?!*" Zelgadiss and Gourry both cried out in surprise.

Lantz raised his thumb up with a wink.

"So that leaves . . ." Zelgadiss shifted his gaze from the heap of berserker and troll corpses near him to a figure with a red silhouette. "*Him*, it would seem . . ."

Gourry emitted an inadvertent groan.

I drew my short sword and silently pressed it against *her* back. "I think it's time to end this charade. Don't you agree, *Eris Vrumugun?*"

Gourry and Zelgadiss snapped to attention at once.

"What?!" Gourry exclaimed.

"What's the meaning of this, Lina?!" Zelgadiss demanded.

For her part, Eris chuckled. "When did you figure it out?" she asked, realizing the gig was up and not making the slightest attempt to deny it.

Her hand, though, did go for the knife at her hip.

"Best if you don't move," I warned. And I meant it.

She ignored my warning and removed her scabbard, tossing it a fair distance.

"Zelgadiss, keep watching 'Rezo' over there," I ordered. "Let me know if he tries anything funny."

Now then . . .

"You tipped your hand when you and Lantz attacked me in the cave," I explained.

"Oh, and how did I do that?" She turned toward me, both fists in her pockets, defiantly.

"Zel came over to rescue me when he heard the sound of my sword slipping from my fingers. So, why didn't Vrumugun stop him from interfering? In order to put those rubies in your foreheads, he had to be nearby. And if he *was* nearby, then why didn't he just finish me off?

"He wouldn't even have needed to face me. A short-range attack spell would've done it.

"So Vrumugun was there to put the rubies on you, but gone by the time Zel came. Either he'd left by a different passageway, which was unlikely, or . . . he was one of you. I knew Lantz from before—"

"But you didn't know me." As she spoke, she brought her left hand up to her brow, where the ruby had been implanted before. "You did get one thing wrong, you know. The ruby in my brow had no effect whatsoever. It would've had to have been a little higher, like on Lantz. No, its purpose was simple camouflage. I needed it to fool Zelgadiss into thinking that I was being controlled as well. But he was too fast, chanting a sleeping spell before I'd noticed. That was my big mistake."

"Seriously?!" Lantz still couldn't believe what he was hearing.

Eris ignored Lantz's outburst and posed another question. "So, what confirmed your suspicions?"

"When Rezo struck Flagohn with magic. If Vrumugun had really spotted us inside the caves, he could've easily left and come back inside with Rezo and all his friends. Also, the aim was a little too accurate. There shouldn't have been any way to target reliably in an echoey cave, which means that someone on our side *had* to have been connected to the Red Priest's consciousness." I pointed to the silent form of our old enemy with my free hand. "You're controlling him through the ruby in his forehead, aren't you? That *impostor.*"

Eris stood there, grinning, betraying no indication of what she was planned to do.

I continued. "Now that I think about it, there were other things. Like when Vrumugun tried to protect you from the man-spider, who likely didn't know that you were allies."

"Well, I wasn't going to gather an army in the name of Erisiel Vrumugun!" She grinned as she continued, "But with my ruby implanted into that *puppet* over there, I could gather legions in the name of Lord Rezo."

She glanced toward her puppet as she spoke, seething with hatred. "You know that my master was blind, don't you? *That* is Lord Rezo's copy homunculus, built as a test subject for Lord Rezo to work on healing his own eyes.

"Though his capacity is certainly great, he lacks a will of his own; he is unable to do anything at all unless I command it." She sighed, almost wistfully.

"No matter how many allies I assembled, it would have been all for naught if you had escaped, wouldn't it? So, pretending to be a bounty hunter, I tailed Zelgadiss from the moment I spotted him.

"Getting hit in the gut wasn't my idea of a good time, but ending up with you—well, I couldn't have planned that better if I'd tried."

"Such is the extent of your eagerness to make your mark as the sorceress who surpassed Rezo the Red Priest," Zelgadiss said while watching over the poor beast who'd been modeled after his former master.

"Oh, sure, there's that, too. But it's really something more," she sighed, looking off into the distance for a moment. "I loved him. Rezo, I mean. The original . . ."

The idea made me nauseous, frankly.

Her hand moved subtly inside her pocket. She pulled something out and flicked it toward me with a finger.

A control ruby!

Plop! It struck my forehead dead center.

"What the—?!"

It wasn't my voice that called out. It was Eris. The ruby bounced right off, falling to the floor at my feet.

"Sorry," I said, smiling and pointing at my forehead. "This is a custommade bandanna." It had been woven from the beard of a black dragon and it was embedded with a small, jeweled talisman at its center. While pressed against my forehead, the talisman acted as a focus for my mental energies while I was casting spells.

And it didn't hurt that it was tough enough to stop a third-rate swordsman's swing cold. Not that I was eager to test it or anything.

"You'll surrender peacefully and void the bounty without a fight, won't you?" I inquired, innocently.

"Hmph!" Eris broke through our encirclement with unexpected speed.

Gourry! Lantz! What were you doing, staring into space?!

"Our battle has only begun!" she cackled. "Come to me, my puppet!"

Upon hearing the voice of his mistress, the standing red silhouette returned to life.

Oh, please. If we were gonna fight here, I wasn't going to waste any time aiming at dolls.

Silently, Rezo's sad experiment maneuvered directly behind his mistress. The bishop's staff in his hand chimed.

Two on five. I'll take those odds.

"Don't underestimate me," Eris groaned. "We're in the middle of Sairaag City. You can't do anything reckless. I will use the welfare of the people as my shield!"

Is it me, or does she sound like a melodramatic villain ratcheting up the wickedness gauge?

"Though he may be a crude clone of the real thing, his capacity is enormous," she offered. "With my expert control, we can more than match the likes of you!"

"No, at this point, you would simply be in the way," said a familiar voice.

"Eh?" Eris spun around, dumbfounded.

THWOOMP! Copy Rezo fired an energy ray that burned straight through Eris' body.

"Gaaahh!" She stared in disbelief at the gaping hole in her gut. She and her puppet then looked each other square in the face.

"Do you find it strange? Do you? That I—a homunculus, a toy—could demonstrate pride? It must seem impossible to you.

"My *pride*, my independent spirit—my soul, if you will—was awakened during *a certain experiment* . . . one that you witnessed yourself."

"Urrhh . . ." Eris moaned. Her knees quivered.

"I cannot fulfill my potential, nor satisfy my pride, as a toy in your service." He spewed resentment with every word. "Did you not think it odd that Vizea so easily became my ally?

"Those of the demon race do not form pacts lightly. They obey only individuals whose power is greater than their own. Did you really think that a Mazoku such as he would mistake me for my master and not detect your charlatanry?

"It seems that like a fool, you never considered it," his voice dripped with disdain. "Well, what Vizea obeyed was *my* power. His pact was with *me*."

The Red Priest removed the control ruby from his forehead with ease, and with the assistance of some unseen force, crushed it between his thumb and forefinger.

"Relaying information to you, running errands back and forth, paying you *respect* . . . I hope you enjoyed it. It must have been *convenient* for you," he hissed.

Eris' knees buckled, her strength depleted. Her former liege reached out and grasped her face with one hand. A weak, plaintive yelp escaped from her lips.

"Now, now . . . not yet. I am far from done with you," he threatened Eris' flaccid form. "Do you understand? Do you understand what all of this is about?"

She did not respond.

"Yes. *Revenge.* In order to experiment with healing magic for the purpose of restoring his own unseeing eyes, Rezo required a copy homunculus, and so he created me.

However, while his experiments resulted in my eyes opening easily, Rezo's remained as useless as ever."

Of course they did. That was because the Red Priest's eyes were sealed shut in order to contain a powerful evil. Though neither that Rezo at the time, nor this Rezo before us now, knew that then.

But if Rezo's experiments were successful, why were his subjects' eyes closed even now?

"Though he did not display it on his face, he was filled with anger, rage, and fierce hatred for me," said Copy Rezo. "He was consumed with jealousy that I, his own flesh and blood, had gained sight, while he remained locked in darkness.

"And so he reused me in a variety of trials in the name of experimental sorcery. And then, during a test that you yourself witnessed, he awakened something within me. Call it my *will*, my *pride* . . .

"I cannot be completely confident that it—any more than anything else—is truly my own. But if it is my own, then perhaps it is simply my hatred that he awoke. My hatred for my master for doing *that*, to me."

Huh?

So, Lord Rezo and his clone didn't dig on each other. That's the gist of it, eh?

But since Rezo was already dead, Vrumugun—that is, Eris—had become the target of his vengeance, which was why he was drawing his speech out so long.

"I have long dreamt of killing Rezo with this very hand. I believed I could defeat even him. But before I could move to realize my desire, my master vanished into thin air. Then," the fake Rezo sighed, "word came of his demise.

"Do you understand, Erisiel? Can you understand the despair I felt then? It should have been by *my* hand that Lord Rezo had fallen. You came to me then, saying that you would use me to avenge our lord. As you called out Rezo's name, sorrow swelled within my breast, and a scheme began to form in my mind.

"I knew I would someday slay you for your part in that experiment, but first—" he suddenly looked concerned. "Erisiel? Are you listening?"

After a long pause, he let go of Eris' face. Her body made a small *plop* as it crumpled to the floor.

It didn't even twitch.

"She is gone." He made a single, offhanded shrug in our direction.

"Fine . . . it's over, then," Gourry said. "Call off the bounty on us. *Now.*"

"Why?" His expression indicated that he had no idea why he should even consider such madness. "My revenge against the Red Priest is not yet complete."

Knew it.

"Rezo's already dead," Gourry said with pity.

Copy Rezo laughed. "Yes, I know. I have no intention of challenging his corpse, should one exist. However, a single method of surpassing Rezo remains."

"To fight and win against us, the people who slew the original," I said.

"Precisely." He nodded.

This is going to be a huge pain in the ass.

He'd let pass his first opportunity to dispose of us, *and* Eris, when we'd first met him face-to-face in the Miasma Forest. Having thrown off Vrumugun's control long before, he could have easily blown us all away by finishing his spell before I'd cast Levitation on the wind barrier.

He didn't. Probably because he had no intention of killing us unless he could say he'd done so when we were at a hundred percent of our power.

My judgment error and our having to take care of Lantz and Eris meant that I hadn't been utilizing all my power. He couldn't surpass the original Rezo by defeating us under those circumstances.

"This is absurd," said Zelgadiss.

"Indeed. I understand how you feel," the fake Red Priest said, sounding genuinely sympathetic. "That is precisely why I have no reason to cancel the bounty now. However, if you defeat me, then the bounty will be lifted, for there will be no one to pay the reward."

His bishop's staff made a small sound as it struck the earth. The chime reverberated.

"Shall we begin?" He smiled.

***

Zelgadiss made the first move, swinging his great broadsword forward.

The duplicate Rezo moved.

The sword's vertical thrust passed by the right flank of its target body. The red mantle fluttered in the wind. Copy Rezo launched a spinning left back kick at Zelgadiss' abdomen then, using the same momentum, followed with a right kick aimed at Zelgadiss' temple.

Somehow Zel managed to dodge both attacks.

"You're kidding me, right?" Zel promptly closed the difference between them and slashed through the momentary opening that the Rezo replica had shown him. A clear, high-pitched sound rang out.

The tip of the clone's staff blocked Zelgadiss' attack. Then, with the hand that bore it acting as a pivot, the staff flew up in the opposite direction, its end thrusting straight into Zelgadiss' gut.

"Wurgh!" Zel's body was blown back with all the force he'd put into his own attack. Copy Rezo had only shown Zelgadiss the opening in order to bait him.

Of course he's that good.

"Come now, take this seriously," the imitation Rezo said, sounding annoyed.

"Wanna try me on for size, then?" Gourry asked. Having quelled the Sword of Light, Gourry raised his bastard sword, still standing near a pile of berserkers he'd likely slain with it.

"I refuse." The fake Rezo shook his head resolutely.

"Gourry, he won't fight you unless you have the Sword of Light," I explained as Gourry stood there, insulted and vaguely confused.

"Precisely."

"Oh fine," Gourry sighed, muttering to himself about how that was no fun as he once again discarded the steel blade of his sword.

"W-wait a minute," Zelgadiss said, rousing himself. "My turn's not done yet."

"As you wish. I will take you on one at a time or as a team, whichever you prefer."

"Don't toy with me!" Zelgadiss yelled out.

Whether with sword or spell, Copy Rezo completely repelled every attack, hand to hand or with a single swing of his staff.

I'm not kidding . . . this guy was *good*. And he had yet to even begin his offense. Individually or all at once, we couldn't afford to hold back a bit.

That said, if I *didn't* hold back on my spells, the city would be turned into a lifeless desert once more.

"Miss Lina," Sylphiel addressed me in a small voice, "I had heard from Mr. Zelgadiss that . . . that you possess the ability to use a spell of even greater power than Dragon Slave."

Giga Slave, she meant.

Hey, what are you doing telling people about that, Zelgadiss?!

Dragon Slave, said to be the most powerful of spells, taps into the power of the Mazoku Lord who holds dominion over all of the chaos of this world—Ruby Eye Shabranigdu. Of course a super-genius sorceress such as myself could use this spell.

Though largely similar to Dragon Slave, Giga Slave is a spell that draws upon the power of the Mazoku Lord of all Mazoku Lords, who governs the entirety of the darkness of all time and space—the Lord of Nightmares.

As an ultra-powerful spell, it naturally had risks. If I lost control of it, the entirety of my life force would likely be absorbed, killing me.

"You absolutely must not use that spell," Sylphiel pleaded.

"Now hold on just a minute," I started. "No one needs to tell me not to use an indiscriminate attack spell like that. I would never use a spell like that in the middle of a city. Not as long as there's another way."

"No, that is not the point at all," Sylphiel interrupted in a strong tone. "I am asking you to never use it again *for the rest of your life.*"

My eyes bulged at the heartfelt request. "But why?"

"Do you know what might happen if you lost control of that spell?" she asked.

Well, not exactly. I'd never known anyone but myself who had ever cast the spell, and I *certainly* hadn't known anyone who'd failed. So, okay, there were a number of things I didn't know about it.

"I'd probably die," I said. I knew that much.

"It is nothing so minor, really."

Minor?! My death is minor *to you?*

"If the prophecy is correct," she said, "then the entire world would be destroyed."

The world . . . would be . . . destroyed?!

"You are aware that prophecy is among the abilities that priestesses possess, yes?"

I nodded.

Prophecy is the ability to commune with gods or other higher beings, to know that which should be unknowable.

Although I'd heard it said to be a useful ability, it was completely outside the control of the person concerned. A priestess had absolutely no idea when, where, or what kind of prophecy would descend upon her. Furthermore, not all prophecies are directly related to matters of significant concern.

For example, if you were to experience a vision of someone sitting on the toilet dreaming up a plot to bring a nation to its knees . . . well, that vision wouldn't be either useful or appetizing, would it? I mean, who's to say that the toilet manifesto would ever come to fruition? You can't fault a man for dreaming while he poops.

Well, that's an extreme case, but you get the point.

However, just because a prophecy concerns a matter of little importance, that does not make it untrue. If you had a prophecy of someone sitting on a toilet dreaming up a plot to bring a nation to its knees, well then, you could be damned certain that somewhere out there someone was sitting on a toilet dreaming up a plot to bring a nation to its knees. Follow?

"Yours is a spell that invites a void into this world," Sylphiel explained. "It is the power to extinguish energy and return matter to nothingness. The bringer of the void becomes its very embodiment. Were you to lose control, then it would not be strange for the world around you to become the embodiment of the void in your place. That's the gist of it, at any rate."

So this is really serious stuff.

I paused in silence for a while and considered the implications.

And, after careful consideration, I decided that this was not the time for serious thought about the matter. I had no intention of using that spell under the present circumstances, prophecy or not.

"Gotcha. I won't use it," I said. Making a promise without due consideration as I was wont to do, I returned my attention to the fight between Zel and the duplicate Rezo once more.

Zelgadiss' breathing was labored, and Copy Rezo was not the slightest bit fazed. The two glared at one another.

It wasn't that Zelgadiss was weak. The Rezo replica was just too strong.

"Damn!" Zelgadiss discarded his sword and began casting a spell.

That spell! Wait!

"Yes, yes! Do it! Lest this all be false," the imitation muttered.

What the hell was he thinking?!

Vlave Howl is a spell to turn a certain area of ground into molten lava. Though it is directional, and therefore wouldn't get those of us behind him tangled up in it, the large section of Sairaag City real estate behind Copy Rezo most certainly would *not* be safe.

Even if it didn't destroy the city outright, the resulting fire certainly would.

"Are you serious, Zel?!"

He turned toward me as I shouted.

"Do you have *any* idea what that'll do to the city if you use it here?!"

"How troublesome," the phony Rezo raised his voice with a tone of dismay, "that you cannot seriously engage me under the circumstances. Defeating you under constraints will have no meaning."

His haughty boasts weren't hot air by any means. I was beginning to think it entirely possible that he possessed greater magical capacity than I did and greater combat capability than Gourry.

"Ah yes! Of course," Copy Rezo grinned. "Then I shall do *this*."

Lit with the same sense of inner glee as a child who just decided to cover the family dog in baking flour and let him run around the house, the replica struck the earth hard with his staff.

"⋀Ⴟ⊢⊌..." Words that were either nonsensical gibberish or some bizarre spell spilled from the Red Priest's lips.

In the next moment, a faintly glittering magic wall enveloped the six of us.

"Wh-what's he trying to do?" Lantz asked no one in particular.

"I am removing the shackles from your feet," the replica replied. "You and Miss Sylphiel are witnesses enough for this battle."

He couldn't mean . . . !

". . . ⊡∏F. . ." The voice began to speak on the wind once more.

"Stop! Please!" I begged.

Too late.

" 王!"

He raised his staff to its zenith, and a dazzlingly bright light tore asunder all that lay beyond the barrier.

The Blessed Blade in Lantz's hand made a sound like a series of tiny pops.

"The hell—!"

"What?! What happened?!"

"What *was* that?!"

I glared at our foe. Only we two understood. At that instant, Sairaag had become the city of death once more.

The light beyond the barrier abated and we began to see.

The first to scream was Sylphiel.

Her anguish echoed around us, drawing attention to the deafening silence of the world outside. While the energy shockwaves our foe had released continued, we heard no sounds from beyond the barrier.

Melon-sized stones blew about like paper, striking one another and crumbling. We couldn't see far, due to sand and smoke, but that wasn't essential to understanding the mystic energy wave's power. It was likely a greater quantity of energy than Dragon Slave. Sairaag City was just . . . gone.

"Impossible," Zelgadiss whispered, his voice hoarse.

Sylphiel collapsed where she stood. Lantz ran to her.

When the smoke around the barrier cleared, the spectacle was even worse than we could have imagined. It was truly a wasteland.

Not a trace remained of the city, its people, their smiles, their joy—nothing that had existed mere moments before.

Only one thing remained . . .

Somehow, Flagohn had survived. Though nothing remained of its thick bark or branches, the bare trunk, like a giant stake, still reached up from the ground.

"Perhaps I overdid it?" the fake Rezo asked. "Well, now you are free to fight with nothing holding you back!" He sounded refreshed.

"D-do you have any idea what you d-did, just now?" I asked, sincerely at a loss.

He smiled tenderly at me as I choked on my words. "I do," he said. "But I don't care. The only matter of concern to me is that you are able to engage me at your full power, so that I may defeat you without conditions—thereby relieving the burden of the ghost of Rezo the Red Priest that still weighs heavily within the depths of my soul."

"I will not aid you in your quest for peace or comfort," I said through gritted teeth. "I'll give you everything I've got, but we will defeat you. And your soul will *burn!*" As I spoke, I brought my hands to my chest and I began chanting a very dark spell.

"Dragon Slave, is it?!" he exclaimed, giddily. Once more, a spell my ears could not comprehend escaped his lips.

Perhaps he was expecting to fire off his spell at me before I'd finished chanting my own, but I wasn't going down easy:

Thou who art darker than night,
Thou who art redder than the flowing blood,
Thou through whom time flows,
I call upon thy exalted name.

I pledge myself to darkness.
Let those fools
Who would oppose us
Suffer destruction
By the power we two possess!

Chaos Words such as those used here govern cause and effect within the world, whereas Power Words release the mental power imprinted within a spellcaster's mind. Just, you know, in case you were wondering. Anyway . . . I completed my spell.

"Dragon Slave!"

"⫟ЕIC!"

Both our spells were released at the same time.

No . . . it's just like before!

The moment I thought that, a deep red mist rose around him where the Dragon Slave spell should have caused a massive explosion.

As he stood there unconcerned, the mist slowly dissipated . . . and that was all.

"Mutual cancellation," he mouthed, disappointed. "I have blocked your Dragon Slave."

I didn't move.

This isn't funny.

That spell was more than capable of destroying powerful Mazoku. No human, not even a great sorcerer, could defend against it.

And yet . . . he did.

"You should not be so surprised," he said flatly, all the giddiness gone. "An attack spell drawing on the power of Ruby-Eye Shabranigdu can be defeated by a defensive spell drawing upon the power of Ruby-Eye Shabranigdu. The theory is not complex."

He spoke as if he were explaining how to make a tuna casserole.

His theory made sense, of course, but Dragon Slave employs the maximum capacity for energy that human beings are capable of. To block it, a defensive spell drawing upon the same power source would require *greater* power than a human can possess!

"Now, then . . ." Rezo's heir calmly raised his staff high as he cast his spell. "⊢!"

Light shot past me.

Gourry dove, and with a flash of the Sword of Light, he somehow blocked the Red Priest's strike.

The staff . . .

"You will be next!" the Red Priest said, his face twitching. A silver light flashed, and the priest's torn red mantle fluttered in the air. Angrily discarding it, the Red Priest moved back a bit, ever closer to Flagohn.

"Sorry for butting in," Zelgadiss said with a smile.

Zel had attacked him from behind without warning— just like a villain.

Then again, considering what our opponent had done to my Dragon Slave, who was I to pick nits about what's fair?

"Zelgadiss!" Gourry chided.

"You're going about this the wrong way, Gourry," Zel said while keeping an eye on the enemy. "He's not an opponent to be taken on fair and square, one on one."

"But . . ."

Treachery in battle was a difficult concept for Gourry.

"Please do come both at once," the Red Priest laughed. "It will be more interesting for me that way. Come, Miss Lina. Will you not join your comrades in this fight?"

I declined.

Don't go around telling people I said this, but while I'm quite confident that my level of swordsmanship is good enough to dispatch a dozen green troops, I couldn't hold a proverbial candle to either Gourry or Zelgadiss. I'd just be slowing them down.

And before you suggest that I could just support them with my magic, remember that keeping track of four bodies in battle gets messy, and I would run risk of hitting one of them by mistake.

"No way," I answered. "I'm brains, not brawn."

"I see. As you wish." He turned to face them both once more.

Of course, I was doing more than playing cheerleader. I was *thinking*. I wasn't coming up with anything, but I was *thinking*, nonetheless.

If he could defend against Dragon Slave, then the only spell I had left was . . .

Giga Slave.

There was no reason that he should know of Giga Slave's existence, so, even if he used the same defensive spell again, Giga was more than powerful enough to break through. However, I would be breaking the promise I made to Sylphiel earlier.

Well, she was still out cold, so she'd never even know I'd used it. Not that that was really the issue.

The three-man battle began just as I was considering my quandary.

The Red Priest had somehow blocked Gourry's blade, leaping back a fair distance while Zelgadiss aimed a spell at him.

"/ʎ\\!" he shouted.

Both voices reverberated, but the splitting air proved louder.

Copy Rezo initiated his first attack. Ten balls of light about the size of a fist instantly appeared around him.

A chill ran down my spine.

That . . . that couldn't be Blast Bomb, could it?!

As far as I knew, only one sorcerer in all recorded history had ever used that spell—Lei Magnus the ancient sage who had invented Dragon Slave. I had once immersed myself in researching the spell, but my effort proved fruitless.

The spell generates multiple miniature balls of fire that explode on impact like fireballs. However, its level of power is in a different class altogether. According to legend, *each* of the balls of light in a Blast Bomb has a destructive power several times that of a fireball.

"Get out of there!" I screamed.

The Red Priest launched the spheres just as I shouted. Gourry and Zel leapt hurriedly, but there wasn't time! The lights exploded in several surging flashes.

Gourry and Zelgadiss were enveloped in crimson flames!

My heart released a silent scream. They had both been utterly consumed. My knees shook as it sunk in.

Gourry . . . Zelgadiss . . .

As the flames and smoke abated, I saw them both standing there, dumbfounded but unharmed.

The Red Priest turned his gaze on me. He was not amused.

No, his gaze wasn't *on* me, it was *behind* me.

"I do not possess the power to defeat you, but I can and must do *something.*"

I turned toward the voice, "Sylphiel!"

Having recovered from her shock, she'd placed a defensive barrier right in front of our boys. It was a pretty intense spell. Her shoulders rose and fell heavily.

"Master Gourry! Master Zelgadiss! I beg you," she screamed, "while the defensive spell still holds, avenge Sairaag City! Avenge my *father!*"

Both men sprang at the Red Priest simultaneously. Zelgadiss launched a spell just out of sword range. Rezo absorbed its power with his left hand. A moment later, his staff sustained Gourry's downward thrust with the Sword of Light.

Then Zelgadiss' broadsword flashed and the Red Priest's body arced. While parrying Gourry's blade, he executed a spinning back kick that slammed into Zelgadiss' wrist, knocking the sword right out of his hand.

Gourry took that opportunity to make another heavy swing with his blade, but the Red Priest blocked with the staff once more.

Zelgadiss, having lost his blade, seemed also to have lost his mind, rushing the Red Priest while armed with nothing but his strength.

The moment their bodies met, a hot flash of light sent Zelgadiss flying back.

"Ugh!" A small groan filtered from his stony lips. However, Zelgadiss smiled as he tried to bring himself back up to standing. His left hand gripped a dagger that he'd hidden somewhere. There was blood on the blade.

The Red Priest turned a hateful glare directly toward Zelgadiss. At that moment, Gourry kicked straight up into Rezo's chin. He leapt for the fallen priest without a moment's hesitation. Gourry's feet came down on the red one's hands, his legs split, the Sword of Light hanging down.

Copy Rezo struggled futilely to push Gourry away, but the Sword of Light batted him back down.

It seemed that the battle would be decided right there . . . without my turn ever arriving.

"Kill him!" Zelgadiss ordered. However, Gourry did not move.

"Swear that you'll cancel the bounty and never come after us again," Gourry demanded as he loomed over Rezo.

"No! Gourry!!" Zelgadiss shouted.

"I don't like to fight like that," Gourry said, "and I don't kill men if I don't have to."

"You do have to," Zel spat, disgusted.

"I am," the Red Priest said, smirking, "stronger than you think!"

For a moment, I thought I heard an echo in his voice.

Gourry flew back as the voice rang out. He went yards before landing . . . no, falling. He rolled several times on impact, red blood spattering on the ground around him.

What the . . . ?

The red silhouette rose slowly.

"No!" Zelgadiss exclaimed involuntarily.

"*This* is what Rezo the Red Priest did to me," the copy began.

Lantz yelled out loud enough to shake the sky. Sylphiel gasped.

And then I saw it—what Rezo had done to his poor creation's face.

His eyelids opened.

Eyelids? No . . . not quite . . .

The sockets were lined with small white growths, while what looked like long, scarlet whips sprung forth from the reddish black darkness within. In all likelihood these were what had ripped into Gourry. I needed a moment to absorb what I was seeing.

It wasn't *eyes* that had opened, really. Where eyes should have been, there were two mouths lined with small, white fangs . . . and they were grinning.

What did he do to you?

The hood he had worn deep over his face was now raised, and a large, vertically opening blue eye stared at us from the creature's forehead.

"Rezo the Red Priest and the sorceress Vrumugun did this to me," one mouth said.

"They fused my body with that of a Mazoku," said the next.

"It was that act that awakened my pride, my will, my *hatred*. There is a certain irony in that, is there not?" The creature's three mouths were conversing with one another.

"I wonder if this pride is my own," the first mouth continued.

"Perhaps it is the Mazoku's pride," offered the second.

"Even *I* know not," said the third.

The blind Red Priest, jealous of his own blood, fused the imitation with a Mazoku. For revenge . . . and likely for amusement as well.

I understood then how the creature was able to command spells of such immense power. They were all techniques that were within the enormous magical capacity of a Mazoku.

Sylphiel said that Flagohn had been growing more rapidly since the creature's arrival. It made sense if you thought about it. The very nature of a Mazoku is extreme hatred. It's not surprising that the evil aura born of that nature would stimulate such growth.

But, in that case . . .

I moved to her side. "Sylphiel," I whispered. "We'll avenge them—your city and your father . . . *I promise.*"

***

"Now then, it's time for the star to take the stage." I advanced slowly.

"Lantz, take care of Gourry," I said, borrowing the Blessed Blade from him as I spoke. "His wounds aren't life-threatening, but he'll need a hand."

The silvery blade had a number of thin cracks running across it—a direct result of its attunement to the newly damaged Flagohn.

I took a look at the Holy Tree.

Hang on, Gourry. This will all be over soon.

"A contest of magic this time?" The creature laughed. "I possess the capacity and capabilities of a Mazoku in recompense for this disgusting body. I give you fair warning: you will lose."

"We won't know unless we try, will we? Let's give it a shot, Zelgadiss."

"Right," Zel answered, tossing aside his dagger.

No dagger would suffice against a creature that was half Mazoku.

"Lina!" Gourry called me over. "Aren't you going to need this?" he asked, offering me the Sword of Light.

"Give it to Zel," I said, raising the Blessed Blade before me. "I'll use this."

"Got it." Gourry smiled and tossed the Sword of Light to Zelgadiss.

"Have you finished your preparations?" the creature asked.

Zel and I nodded.

"⊢!" Rezo's three mouths chanted separate spells simultaneously.

A Mazoku's capacity and hybridized spell-casting . . .

We leapt. Blue plasma rushed along the surface of the earth. We would have fallen prey to it had we not jumped. I finished my spell the moment we touched ground.

"Goz Vu Rou!"

A black shadow advanced along the ground toward the creature. He would sustain damage directly from the astral side if it reached him.

We can win this . . .

"That is futile!" the creature said as he raised his staff, preparing to smash the shadow as he had before.

Not so fast, you freak . . .

SNAP!

I created a large wave as I snapped my fingers. The shadow altered course accordingly. The creature understood Goz Vu Rou as a directional spell, and normally it would be, but a minor modification was possible.

"What?!" The creature leapt back. The shadow stubbornly pursued.

"... b!"

He traced an arc over the ground with the tip of his staff as he cast his spell.

Phzzt! The shadow was neatly wiped out as it came into contact with the circle.

Zelgadiss seized the opportunity and lunged for the creature's flank. The creature pulled back, unperturbed, as the Sword of Light flashed.

Zel charged the creature again. A new blade of light sprang from the hilt in his hand. He meant to slash with the sword while the creature's staff was still recovering from the first attack.

The creature, however, knocked the magic blade away with his bare hand, swinging his staff at Zel!

Clang! Zelgadiss was hit squarely and blown back hard.

I'd circled around behind him, my spell nearly complete. Sensing this, the creature hurriedly chanted a counter . . . but I was faster.

"Dynast Brass!"

Lightning rained down around the creature in the form of a pentagram. No sooner had it formed than the fire bolts began closing in, assailing him from all sides.

The creature raised his staff as he completed his spell. But then . . .

Crack! His staff noisily disintegrated.

Likely, between my attack spell and the creature's defensive energy, it simply could not take the strain.

The lightning struck the creature squarely!

"Gaaaaaah!" all three mouths cried at once.

The pentagram symbol blew apart. He'd countered my spell with the force of his raw mental power alone.

"Not bad," the creature said, giving me my due.

Zel, now recovered, lunged in for another attack, missing the creature but forcing him farther back toward Flagohn. There, the creature began to chant anew.

Since we had no idea what spell was coming, our only option was to get out of its way. But since we didn't know if would be a surface spell or an air attack, how could we evade?

Dammit.

I remained fixed on the ground, my stomach in knots. It was pointless trying to read the creature without understanding what made him tick. I had to trust my gut.

"Ϲ!" The creature opened his arms wide as he completed his spell.

A dazzling light shot out from his body. There wasn't even time to shout. The white light hit Zel and me at full force.

When it was done, I dropped to my knees where I stood. From what I could tell, Zelgadiss was in the same condition. I raised a hand toward Gourry and Lantz as they looked on, concerned. Sylphiel was nowhere to be seen. She'd apparently left during the fight.

Well then, time to put our end in order.

I rose to my feet. "You okay, Zel?"

I raised the Blessed Blade. The creature stood between the weapon and Flagohn.

The spell that had wiped us out was some kind of large-scale Elmekia Lance. It inflicted damage directly to the mind, temporarily weakening an opponent's mental faculties.

When I said *large-scale,* I was referring to its range rather than its force. Instead of the usual spear of light, this version shot out a huge light wave. Of course, that came at the sacrifice of power. One hit wasn't enough to cripple the nervous system to the point of collapse, but our powers were considerably weakened. No matter how hard I might try, getting off a big spell was going to be iffy.

Zelgadiss was in the exact same situation. The Sword of Light's blade, the physical manifestation of the wielder's power, had shortened considerably.

"Anyway, let's do it!" I said, breaking into a run.

Zelgadiss reluctantly followed.

I was fully aware that the creature could easily handle the few clumsy stunts that we were capable of producing in that condition. While it was possible that we could strike him down with the Blessed Blade and the Sword of Light, the creature's hand-to-hand skills were greater than Zelgadiss' or mine.

We both swung our swords simultaneously as we rushed past the creature. He easily deflected our blows and launched a spinning back kick at Zelgadiss, which Zel somehow evaded by a hair's breadth. We regrouped at the base of Flagohn's bare trunk.

"What do we intend to do?" Zel asked. "Or do you just do, without intending?"

"On my signal," I said, "Nail him with a fireball and peel off to the side."

"Understood." Zelgadiss didn't say another word.

"Let's do it!" I said, and I took off running once more.

If we don't settle this here . . .

"It is time to bring this to an end," Copy Rezo said, extending both hands out to us.

"Zel!"

On my signal . . .

Zelgadiss fired several balls of light at the creature in rapid succession.

"Haa!" The Red Priest waved his left hand up, causing a great explosion in midair. He'd destroyed the fireballs with directly channeled magical energy. Flashes and smoke clouded our field of vision, but the creature's eye saw through the obstructions.

"Weak!" the creature scoffed.

He gathered a spell in his hand, shooting it at the spot I'd been a moment ago, before I'd moved to his rear.

He either sensed my movement, or my presence, and he turned his head back. But it was too late. I was right in front of his face.

With my wind spell coiled around the Blessed Blade, I released the sword. It thrust forward like a spear, plunging straight into the creature's chest!

"Gwaaah!" Copy Rezo screamed. The blade sunk deep into him down to the hilt, the force impaling his body upon Flagohn behind him.

When the fireballs were exploding, I'd used Ray Wing to fly over the creature's head and come back down behind him.

Finished!

"Not yet!" Zelgadiss yelled.

"You think *this* is enough to finish me?" The creature grasped the sword he was impaled upon.

With the Blessed Blade out of my hands, it was nowhere near enough to affect his demonic vitality. However . . .

"Sylphiel!" I shouted. She had been waiting behind Flagohn for her turn to act.

Creeeaaak.

The Holy Tree pulsed heavily. Its creaking blended with the creature's moans to fill the wasteland that Sairaag had become.

Sylphiel had cast a spell upon Flagohn under my direction. It was a common spell, one used to boost the life force and speed the natural healing process of the being upon whom it was cast.

Twig by twig, Flagohn's lost bark, branches and leaves began to regrow. For this, a great deal of energy was required. There was a source close at hand, a powerful source of miasma—Copy Rezo.

Flagohn continued to recover at a rapid rate. Its thick bark was regenerating before our eyes, with stalks sprouting from it left and right. Leaves grew into branches in the twinkle of an eye.

The creature continued to moan steadily. The miasma, the source of the Mazoku's vitality, was being drained from

him. The tree was *consuming* the Mazoku part of the creature. All that remained was his humanity. But, with his chest wound . . .

Copy Rezo coughed and spat out blood.

"H-how?" he moaned in a small voice. "How did I . . . how did I lose? Why could I . . . not . . . surpass my master?"

"You don't see it?" My question made him fall silent for a time.

"I . . . I never saw beyond his back. That is why . . ."

"Yes," I whispered.

Whoosh.

Wind echoed through the lush leaves of Flagohn.

The creature coughed up more blood.

"What name shall we inscribe on your grave?" Zelgadiss asked.

"That is not necessary," the creature smiled in reply. "This tree . . . shall be my tombstone." That said, he left our world with a sigh.

. . . And lush green treetops swayed with the wind.

"There really are a lot of guards around here," I said, nibbling on some lamb. We were at an inn close to Saillune City, the capital of the Holy Kingdom of Saillune (what made it *holy* was beyond me).

"Saillune's a pretty stuffy place, isn't it?" I asked rhetorically.

"Well, if things go well, we'll get there tomorrow," Gourry said. He had a drumstick in each hand.

"Thank you very much for everything," Sylphiel interjected. She sounded refreshed. "I'm sorry for all the trouble.

"Master Gourry, thank you for escorting me all this way," she said, then turning to me, added, "and Miss Lina, thank you as well."

"Hey, you helped us out a lot too, remember," Gourry said, grinning. Well, *that* was true.

After we had put the Sairaag incident in order, Sylphiel, who'd surely taken the worst mental beating of any of us, shook it off pretty well. Of course, she'd done some crying and a lot of throwing up. Then she traveled with us to the next city over and helped with the formalities of having the bounty lifted.

Having lost her home, she'd decided to travel to Saillune City and rely on relatives there. Since the passage was dangerous, she asked that we act as her bodyguards on the trip.

I didn't want to accept that invitation, honestly. I've harbored a strong dislike for Saillune's First Royal Heir to the Throne (don't call him *Prince*, even by mistake) ever since I'd met him.

For anyone else, I would have refused, but for Sylphiel . . .

Lantz split off along the way to travel alone. "I don't think I'm gonna live long around you people," he said. "No offense."

None taken.

Zelgadiss reported that he was going to "search for the means to revert to a human body." There might have been a method in Saillune for all I knew, but when I invited him along, Zel refused. He thought it was a bad idea for some reason or other.

I wonder how those two are doing.

When I thought back on it, there was one scene from the Sairaag affair that stood out in my mind: Flagohn, silently waving in the wind in the center of the wasteland. And there, at its base, the nameless man to whom Rezo the Red Priest had given both life and the burden of his twisted existence slept . . . with a cracked and shabby sword in place of a tombstone.

Hajime Kanzaka + "L"

Author: H-hello. Author here.

AUTHOR GLANCES OVER SHOULDER WARILY.

L: Stop squirming. I didn't bring Minion **S** with me this time.

A: R-really?

AUTHOR REMAINS WARY.

L: Yes, really.

A: Um—er—so, you've figured out that those off-the-record attacks don't work, right? Okay, then! Nothing to be worried about at all.

L'S FACE TWITCHES SLIGHTLY.

L: A-anyway, congratulations on your third published work.

A: Oh, that's thanks to all the nice readers out there. Thankyouthankyou!

[THAT REALLY IS WHAT THE AUTHOR THINKS, ALL KIDDING ASIDE.]

L: I see. I think that if they knew how often you yell "Oh no!" every time someone points out a boo-boo while you're writing, they'd drop you like a hot potato.

A: Er . . . Eep.

L: Ah, speaking of boo-boos, you said Dragon Slave's a spell using a person's max capabilities, but Lina fired off one after the other in *Dragon Magazine*.

A: Ah, *that*. Using all of a person's capacity isn't like using up all your MP at once like in a video game. It's like the maximum-size bucket you can use to take water out of a pool. Giga Slave *does* drain all the MP, though.

L: Pretty suspicious explanation, isn't it?

A: Heh. Don't think about it too much.

L: Um okay, next question. Silent Split's . . .

A: Uh, no . . .

L: Argh! This is turning into a game FAQ or something!

A: Please don't put it like that . . .

L: So! Anyway, it's time again for **L**'s bizarre and popular Readership Contest Event Corner. Last time it was the author's Y/M/D of birth. This time . . .

A: You're doing it again?

L: Hey . . . it's popular . . .

A: It is that. But I tend to spontaneously self-destruct when I see the mountain of replies out of nowhere. On that note, sorry I had to stop taking applications last time.

L: Oh, by the way, the answer was 19640717. I think that was harder than the sphinx or da Vinci.

A: I'm older than the winds of chaos, huh?

L: Now then, next question . . .

A: Wait a minute! Let me see that question sheet!

AUTHOR RIPS SHEET OUT OF L'S HAND.

Multiple choice question: Who's the main character of the Slayers series?

1) Lina __verse 2) Hom __ni 3) Fus ____n

The first one hundred thousand people getting the answers right get handwritten replies from the author?!

L: Er, well, I guess making it multiple choice is a bit unusual.

A: Uh, yeah . . .

L: Well two are pretty obviously wrong.

A: Aaaaaah! What are you doing putting a bounty out on my head like this?!

L: Jeez, it's not like that at all.

A: Maybe not . . . but what's this *first one hundred thousand respondents* thing?!

L: Well, I wanted to please the readers.

A: Oh really! Even if it's gonna KILL ME, is that it?!

Hey, all you readers! DO NOT ANSWER THAT LAST QUESTION! PLEASE!!!

L: Bummer . . . so, how 'bout a fanart contest instead?

A: Well, that's all right, I guess.

L: OKAY, we'll do the painting contest! Pro or amateur, young or old, fully grown thirteen seconds after birth, four-hundred-years old, or super-cute main characters, all may apply!

All paintings with magic charms embedded in them WILL be disqualified.

You may paint on any material, but stained glass will be disqualified. Also, don't ship over anything that's too big for Mr. Publisher to handle.

A: Um, is this all right? Without even asking anyone . . .

L: How would I know? Anyway, the subject for painting's any character *who hasn't been drawn* in *Dragon Magazine* or the novels.

A: Now just wait a darn—! How can you paint *them*?

L: Hey. If it were normal, it'd be boring. You can draw people who've only been seen in silhouette, though. We're not turning anyone away, no matter how good or bad the results. We'll use our subjective judgment and give it to Mr. Author one a month as a present. Whether he uses it for a collection or as toilet paper is up to him . . .

A: Hmm. Really laying the gauntlet down to the readers I see. Is it really okay to be doing this?

L: I told you, I have no idea. Well, anyway, this includes characters like Zorom, durahans, Daymia and Rithahn, proper portraits of Rod and Rodimus, non-mummy Zolf, and so on.

Maybe the dragroll (troll-dragon) from Atlas City, too.

Stuff like Seigram's face (w/o mask) and the Water Dragon Lord (footprint only) are against the rules. Of course, if you really wanna win, you can draw your friendly neighborhood "**L**"! (Make me pretty, of course.)

. . . Anyway, isn't it time for me to take a stab at writing?

A: Like hell!

L: Why not? I could end the series in thirty pages if you let me!

A: Aaaah! That's why I'm not letting you!

L: *What was that?*

[THE FOLLOWING SCENE WAS OMITTED DUE TO BARBARITY EXCEEDING THE BOUNDS OF COMMUNITY STANDARDS.]

L: Hmm, it seems that the author is unable to continue due to a flare-up in the symptoms of his chronic illness. I apologize on his behalf.

Well, guess this is the conclusion . . .

Thank you all very much.

IN THE NEXT VOLUME...

Slayers

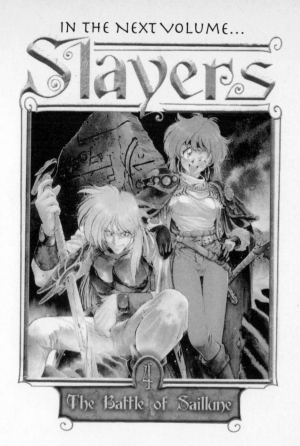

4
The Battle of Saillune

It seems our little band of adventurers just can't catch a break. Employed as guards, Lina and Gourry accompany Sylpheel to Saillune City. Unfortunately, the royal family feud is downright deadly. Can they help Prince Philionel survive assassination attempts and keep their own heads on straight? When you've got the deadliest hunters, dark sorcerers, bug-like monsters, and other grotesque creatures on your tail, it's going to take a little sorceress with some major magical power and a swordsman with phenomenal abilities and a lot of luck to save the day. Onward!

TOKYOPOP SHOP

WWW.TOKYOPOP.COM/SHOP

HOT NEWS!

Check out the
TOKYOPOP SHOP!
The world's best
collection of manga in
English is now available
online in one place!

WARCRAFT

SLAYERS MANGA NOVEL

THE TAROT CAFÉ

- LOOK FOR SPECIAL OFFERS
- PRE-ORDER UPCOMING RELEASES!
- COMPLETE YOUR COLLECTIONS

SOKORA REFUGEES™

Kana thought life couldn't get any worse—behind on her schoolwork and out of luck with boys, she is also the only one of her friends who hasn't "blossomed." When she falls through a magical portal in the girls' shower, she's transported to the enchanted world of Sokora—wearing nothing but a small robe! Now, on top of landing in this mysterious setting, she finds that her body is beginning to go through some tremendous changes.

Preview the manga at:
www.TOKYOPOP.com/sokora

T
TEEN
AGE 13+

HYPER POLICE
BY MEE

In a future rife with crime, humans are an endangered species—and monsters have taken over! Natsuki is a cat girl who uses magical powers to enforce the law. However, her greatest threat doesn't come from the criminals. Her partner Sakura, a "nine-tailed" fox, plots to eat Natsuki and gobble up her magic! In this dog-eat-dog world, Natsuki fights to stay on top!

OT OLDER TEEN AGE 16+

© MEE

LAGOON ENGINE
BY YUKIRU SUGISAKI

From the best-selling creator of *D·N·Angel!*

Yen and Jin are brothers in elementary school—and successors in the Ragun family craft. They are Gakushi, those who battle ghosts and evil spirits known as "Maga" by guessing their true name. As Yen and Jin train to join the family business, the two boys must keep their identities a secret...or risk death!

T TEEN AGE 13+

© Yukiru SUGISAKI

PhD: PHANTASY DEGREE
BY HEE-JOON SON

Sang is a fearlessly spunky young girl who is about to receive one hell of an education...at the Demon School Hades! She's on a mission to enroll into the monsters-only class. However, monster matriculation is not what is truly on her mind—she wants to acquire the fabled "King's Ring" from the fiancée of the chief commander of hell!

T TEEN AGE 13+

© SON HEE-JOON, DAIWON C.I. Inc.